WHAT EVERY CHRISTIAN SHOULD KNOW ABOUT THE TRINITY

How the Bible Reveals One God in Three Persons

ROB PHILLIPS

Missouri Baptist Press

Copyright © 2019 by Rob Phillips

All rights reserved. No part of this book may be reproduced, stored in a retrieval system, or transmitted in any form or by any means, except for brief quotations in critical reviews or articles, without the prior written permission of the author.

Unless otherwise indicated, Scripture quotations are from the Christian Standard Bible (2017).

Executive editor: Dr. John Yeats

Theological review: Robert M. Bowman Jr.

Cover design and graphics: Katie Shull

Layout: Brianna Boes

Production management: Leah England

Kindle production: Brianna Boes

Scripture verification: Christie Dowell

Proofreading: Christie Dowell, Nancy Phillips

CONTENTS

Foreword	v
Introduction	ix
Chapter One: Defining the Trinity	1
Chapter Two: False Views of the Trinity	15
Chapter Three: One God	27
Chapter Four: Three Persons	43
Chapter Five: The Father is God	61
Chapter Six: The Son is God	79
Chapter Seven: Jesus as the God-Man	113
Chapter Eight: The Holy Spirit is God	133
Chapter Nine: The Trinity and Creation	151
Chapter Ten: The Trinity and Salvation	167
Chapter Eleven: The Trinity and Scripture	185
Chapter Twelve: Subordination and Scripture	207
Closing Thoughts	233
Notes	235
Additional Resources	247

FOREWORD

Robert M. Bowman Jr.

A book on the Trinity? You might be wondering if this will be like a book teaching "the new math." What, are you going to try to explain to me that three is one and one is three? To many people, the Trinity is nothing more than a mathematical puzzle or absurdity, something the early church invented to make Christianity harder to believe. Nothing could be further from the truth.

In this book, you will learn that the doctrine of the Trinity is biblical, meaningful, and practical.

First, **the doctrine of the Trinity is biblical**. Of course, the word *Trinity* is not used in any of the books of the Bible. However, the doctrine is biblical because all of the essential elements of the doctrine are clearly taught in the Bible. Indeed, as you will learn as you work through this book, the core truths of the doctrine of the Trinity are found throughout the New Testament. The doctrine simply teaches us how to think about the Father, the Son, and the Holy Spirit in a way that is faithful to what the New Testament says about them. You might be surprised how much of the New Testament touches on the subject in one way or another.

Second, **the doctrine of the Trinity is meaningful**.

It isn't nonsense or a mathematical contradiction. It tells us important truths about the nature of God and about what he is doing in the world. It helps us view the Son and the Holy Spirit as fully divine – as sharing in the essential nature or character of the Creator – while not making the mistake of thinking that Jesus is the Father or that the Holy Spirit is Jesus in another form. Studying the doctrine of the Trinity will not enable you to comprehend God fully or exhaustively. We will never have such complete understanding of God in our lifetimes! Even such a seemingly simple concept as God being eternal boggles our limited minds. However, studying the doctrine will clarify a great deal for you and help you to keep important truths straight. In turn, understanding the doctrine of the Trinity will help you grasp more clearly what the Bible says about the Father, Son, and Holy Spirit. This book won't eliminate the mystery, but it will help you understand what you need to know in order to appreciate our mysterious, wonderful Creator.

Third, **the doctrine of the Trinity is practical.** Understanding the persons of the Father, Son, and Holy Spirit turns out to be important to our experience in living out the Christian life as followers of Jesus Christ. All three persons perform essential roles in our salvation, roles that are best understood in the context of the Trinity. The doctrine helps us to understand why we rightly direct our prayers and worship both to God the Father and to the Lord Jesus, as well as what role the Holy Spirit plays in our worship. Jesus came to invite us into a communion of love with the Father and himself through the presence of the Holy Spirit. In a sense, the doctrine of the Trinity is all about love – the love of the Father and the Son for one another, the love that they show toward us through the Holy Spirit, and how their love is both the model and the source for the love that we are called to show toward one another. What could be more important?

This book on the Trinity does two things that are especially valuable for Christians seeking to live faithfully in this often confusing world. First, it carefully explains how *the doctrine of the Trinity intersects with other areas of Christian belief.* First and foremost, the doctrine is crucial to our understanding of Jesus Christ. Who is Jesus? This question cannot be answered adequately without addressing the issues pertaining to the Trinity. The doctrine of the Trinity provides the "backstory" to the coming of Jesus Christ into the world for our salvation. It is the story of the Father sending his Son to die for our sins and rise from the dead to obtain eternal life for us. It is also the story of the Father and the Son sending the Holy Spirit to bring us to repentance and faith, to bring us from spiritual death to spiritual life, and to bring us from immaturity to maturity as believers. Just as all three persons are intimately involved in our salvation, we learn from the New Testament that all three persons were actively involved in the creation of the world and in the inspiration of Scripture through which we learn about all these things. There really is no area of essential Christian doctrine that is not affected by how we view the Father, Son, and Holy Spirit.

The other important thread running through this book is *the contrast between the biblical, sound Christian doctrine of the Trinity and the false doctrines being taught by various religious groups today.* It is difficult to appreciate the importance of a true doctrine until you contrast it with the false alternatives that are being taught. For example, what happens when a religious group rejects the historic Christian belief that Jesus Christ is God the Son, the second person of the Trinity? They don't just bypass the issue of who or what Jesus is; rather, they come up with their own idea:

- Unitarians maintain that Jesus did not exist in heaven before his human life on earth, but instead was created in the womb of the virgin Mary, lived

as a perfect man, was raised from the dead, and was exalted to heaven as a semi-divine being.
- Mormonism teaches that Christ is the first spirit son of a heavenly Father and a heavenly Mother, who were our spiritual parents in heaven before we were born as physical beings on the earth.
- Jehovah's Witnesses claim that Jesus Christ was originally Michael the archangel, a super-angel that God created and later sent as a perfect man (but no more than that) to die and then become re-created as an angel.

By explaining the differences between these (and other) false doctrines and what the Bible teaches, this book brings into focus why the doctrine of the Trinity matters.

I heartily recommend this book. You will be instructed, illuminated, and encouraged in your Christian faith as you work through its chapters.

> "The grace of the Lord Jesus Christ,
> and the love of God,
> and the fellowship of the Holy Spirit,
> be with you all."

2 Corinthians 13:14 (NASB)

INTRODUCTION

Would it surprise you to know that six out of ten U.S. adults say the Holy Spirit is a force, not a personal being? Or, more shocking, that seventy-eight percent of Americans with "evangelical beliefs"[1] agree with the statement that Jesus was the first and greatest being created by God the Father? These views, part of Ligonier Ministries' 2018 State of Theology survey of three thousand Americans, expose the soft underbelly of evangelical Christianity in our country.[2] If Jesus is God's first and greatest created being, then Arius, the fourth-century heretic, was right after all. On the other hand, if Jesus is the uncreated, eternal Son of God, then the church has made little headway in promoting sound doctrine since the councils of Nicaea and Constantinople pushed back against Arianism.

There's little doubt that the doctrine of the Trinity is mysterious. Some would say it's mind-boggling, or that it violates logic. After all, it claims that God is three and yet one. How is this possible? Charles Taze Russell, founder of the Watch Tower Bible and Tract Society, rejected the Trinity as unreasonable. Joseph Smith, who established the Church of Jesus Christ of Latter-day Saints, redefined the Godhead and urged his followers to pursue their own destinies as gods. Other counterfeit forms of Christianity, as well as some Christian sects, use the term *Trinity* but fail to define it biblically.

So, it's important for followers of Jesus to understand, as best we can, the triune God who created us, loves us, and redeemed us. There are a number of reasons for this. First, from a historical perspective, the Trinity was the first doctrine that the church felt it necessary to explain in a definitive way at the councils of Nicaea (AD 325) and Chalcedon (AD 381). This set orthodox Christianity apart from heretical movements like Docetism, which challenged the church as early as the first century.

Next, the doctrine of the Trinity distinguishes orthodox Christianity from other monotheistic religions such as Judaism and Islam. It also separates Christianity from polytheistic and pantheistic religions like Hinduism and Buddhism.

Third, a proper understanding of the triune God builds a solid foundation for other Christian doctrines, such as creation and redemption. How is it that the Father, Jesus, and the Holy Spirit all are depicted as actively involved in the *ex nihilo* (out of nothing) creation of everything, both visible and invisible – and yet, "In the beginning God created the heavens and the earth" (Gen. 1:1)? Further, how can it be that the second person of the Godhead took on human form, without abandoning His deity, in order to bear our sins on the cross – an offering the Father accepted for our justification and the Spirit applied in bringing new life to believing sinners? Our view of the Trinity affects many other doctrines of Scripture as well.

Rather than view the doctrine of the Trinity as a stumbling block to belief, we should explore the triune God and enjoy the majesty and the mystery of this one divine being who has eternally existed as three co-equal, loving, selfless persons in whose image we are created.

In the pages that follow, we present the doctrine of the Trinity as simply and faithfully to Scripture as possible, providing questions at the end of each chapter for further study. We begin in Chapter One with a simple definition of the Trinity, moving on to false definitions and analogies in Chapter Two. In Chapter Three, we show how the Bible is clear that there is only one true God. Then, in Chapters Four through Eight, we see how Yahweh exists as three distinct, but inseparable, co-equal, co-eternal persons: Father, Son, and Holy Spirit. In Chapter Nine, we view the Trinity in creation, and in Chapter Ten, we see how the Father, Son, and Holy Spirit work together to secure our redemption. In Chapter Eleven, we trace the fingerprints of the Godhead on the development of Scripture. Finally, Chapter Twelve addresses the issue of subordination – how the co-equal members of the Godhead relate with and submit to one another.

Whether you use this resource for personal or group study, our prayer is that it strengthens your confidence in the one true God who is greater than all, who fashioned you to be His imager, and who condescended to adopt you as His son or daughter to enjoy everlasting fellowship as a joint heir of all things with Jesus.

The persons of the Trinity may be distinguished but never separated.

CHAPTER ONE

Defining the Trinity

How do you biblically define a term that never appears in the Bible? As Jehovah's Witnesses, Muslims, and others are quick to point out, the word *Trinity* is conspicuously absent from the pages of Scripture. Therefore, they argue, to embrace such a term goes against the Bible's clear teaching.

Not so fast. While it's true that *Trinity* is not found in English Bible translations, that doesn't mean the doctrine is missing in action. We might point out that phrases such as "the second coming" and "receiving Jesus as Savior" never grace the Bible's pages either. Even so, Christians look forward to the return of Jesus one day, and we enjoy benefits as adopted children of God, having received Him by faith (John 1:12).

So, when we talk about the Trinity, it's important to show how Scripture describes God as one eternal being in three persons. This is not as easy as it sounds, for the Trinity in some respects is a mystery – a revelation of God hidden in times past but revealed progressively from Genesis to Revelation.

J. I. Packer writes, "The historic formulation of the Trinity seeks to circumscribe and safeguard this mystery (not explain it; that is beyond us), and it confronts us with perhaps the most difficult thought that the human mind has ever been asked to handle. It is not easy; but it's true."[1]

Efforts to make God more understandable by reducing Him to a monolithic being actually diminish His character. Think about it: If God is the Creator of everything; if He is sovereign over the universe; if He is all-powerful, all-knowing, and everywhere present at the same time; if He exists outside of time and yet operates within it; if He owns the cattle on a thousand hills and yet became poor for our sake in the person of Jesus Christ; if He authors Scripture without dictating it, but by enabling sinful and fallen men to use their unique insights and experiences to pen the very words of God; then, in some respects, it's foolish to think we can squeeze the Divine Sovereign into skinny jeans.

As physical beings living in a physical universe, we may be tempted to confine our view of reality to the natural realm. But as Freddy Davis points out, "[T]here is a part of reality which exists beyond the physical universe. If we are to know anything about these transcendent matters, they must somehow be revealed to us by someone who lives in that transcendent reality. As such, the things which have their foundation in eternity are not things which can be observed and manipulated using observation and experimental science."[2]

Davis goes on to say, "The Trinity is one of those things which has its foundation in the eternal spiritual world and cannot be demonstrated by natural science. In fact, a Trinity cannot even exist based on the laws of the material universe. When we get to the bottom line, the only reason we even know anything about it is because God has revealed this to us."[3]

There are many mysteries in the Bible that Christians embrace as true without fully understanding them. Take divine election – the unfathomable work in which God's sovereignty and human responsibility meet in salvation so that God does as He pleases and human beings are held fully accountable for their actions. Or consider the Incarnation – God becoming flesh in the person of Jesus of Nazareth. Or regeneration – the unseen work of the Holy Spirit that breathes new life into our dead spirits. Even the kingdom of heaven is a mystery that Jesus sought to explain in nearly two dozen parables. None of these great doctrines is diminished by its complexity. In fact, God is magnified as we explore His great work before time, in time, and beyond time.

Some critics of the Trinity attack the doctrine precisely because of its complexity. Muslims, for example, are taught from childhood to reject the Trinity, in part because it's too complicated. Yet even they must admit that the wonder, vastness, and intricate design of the universe humble even the brightest minds. So, why must we assume the Creator is any simpler, or easier to understand, than the creation?

The late Nabeel Qureshi, a former Muslim who came to faith in Christ, once wrote, "By definition, we cannot comprehend God. If God created our minds, then he must be greater than their comprehension. Who are we to demand that he be simple enough for us to understand him?"[4]

A SIMPLE DEFINITION

Let's begin with a simple definition of the Trinity. The word comes from the Latin *trinitas*, meaning "threeness." We may rightly say the Trinity is a term used to describe the one true and living God, who exists as three distinct, but inseparable, co-equal, co-eternal persons – Father, Son, and Holy Spirit. As *The Baptist Faith & Message* explains, "The eternal triune God reveals Himself to us as Father, Son, and Holy Spirit, with distinct personal attributes, but without division of nature, essence, or being."[5]

Theologian Bruce Ware lays out the traditional view of the Trinity: "[T]here is one and only one God, eternally existing and fully expressed in three Persons, the Father, the Son, and the Holy Spirit." At the same time, "each member of the Godhead is equally God, each is eternally God, and each is fully God – not three gods but three Persons of the one Godhead." Further, "each possesses fully the identically same, eternal divine nature, yet each is also an eternal and distinct personal expression of the one undivided divine nature."[6]

While it's challenging to fully grasp the doctrine of the Trinity, it may advance our understanding to distinguish between *being* and *person*. As Nabeel Qureshi explains, "Your being is the quality that makes you *what* you are, but your person is the quality that makes you *who* you are."[7] For example, if someone asks who you are, you don't reply, "I'm a human being." You respond by sharing your name, which identifies you as a person.

When we say God is a Trinity, we are describing the *what* of God. When we speak of the Father, Son, and Holy Spirit, we are referring to the *who* of God – three persons, indivisible in substance and nature, but distinct in identity.

Qureshi continues, "God ... is one being, Yahweh, in three persons: Father, Son, and Spirit. He's more than able to exist like that because he is God. If we say God must have only one person, like humans, then we are making God in our image. Who are we to limit God? It is up to God to tell us who he is."[8]

Freddy Davis notes, "The Father, Son, and Holy Spirit are all part of the single being who is God, but are also three separate centers of consciousness within that single God who are able to interact with one another in a legitimate personal relationship."[9]

As we prepare to delve more deeply into the doctrine of the Trinity, let's consider three simple truths taught in Scripture:

1. There is only one true God.
2. The Father is God; the Son is God; and the Holy Spirit is God.
3. The Father, Son, and Holy Spirit are distinct, but inseparable, persons who exist simultaneously.

There is only one true God. Christians do not worship three gods; that's polytheism. We do not worship one God made up of three parts; that's tritheism. Nor do we exalt God as one person who wears three different masks; that's modalism.

We do not worship a "freakish-looking, three-headed god," as Jehovah's Witnesses charge; that's just silly.[10]

Rather, Christians worship one God who exists as three distinct, co-equal, co-eternal persons, sharing all the attributes of deity, agreeing completely in will and purpose, and existing eternally in divine, loving relationships with one another.

Scripture is clear that there is only one true and living God. The *Shema*, the most important text for considering Jewish monotheism, reads, "Listen, Israel: The Lord our God, the Lord is one" (Deut. 6:4). The Lord Himself declares in Isaiah 43:10, "No god was formed before me, and there will be none after me." And the apostle Paul writes, "there is one God who will justify the circumcised by faith and the uncircumcised through faith" (Rom. 3:30).

Many other passages could be cited, but there is a clear and consistent theme throughout Scripture that there is one, and only one, true God.

The Father is God; the Son is God; and the Holy Spirit is God. In hundreds of Scripture passages, the Father, Son, and Holy Spirit are declared to be the true God. A few examples:

Father. Paul writes, "yet for us there is one God, the Father. All things are from him, and we exist for him" (1 Cor. 8:6).

In his first epistle, Peter writes, "Blessed be the God and Father of our Lord Jesus Christ. Because of his great mercy he has given us new birth into a living hope through the resurrection of Jesus Christ from the dead" (1 Pet. 1:3).

Son. In Hebrews 1:8, the Father, speaking to the Son, says, "Your throne, O God, is forever and ever, and the scepter of your kingdom is a scepter of justice."

Throughout the New Testament, we see that Jesus exhibits the attributes of God. He is eternal (John 1:1). He has all authority (Matt. 28:18). He is unchanging (Heb. 13:8). Further, He is the Creator (John 1:3; Col. 1:16). He forgives sin, receives worship, and claims equality with the Father (Mark 2:5; John 10:30; 20:28; Heb. 1:6).

Holy Spirit. Called the Spirit of God and the Spirit of Christ (Rom. 8:9; 1 Pet. 1:11), the Holy Spirit is revealed as both divine and personal. For example, when Ananias lies to the Holy Spirit, Peter points out, "You have not lied to people but to God" (Acts 5:4).

Time and time again, as we read through the Bible, particularly the New Testament, we see that the one true and living God (one *being*) exists in three *persons*: Father, Son, and Holy Spirit.

The Father, Son, and Holy Spirit are distinct, but inseparable, persons who exist simultaneously. The false doctrine of modalism teaches that God reveals Himself consecutively as Father, Son, and Holy Spirit. But Scripture paints a much different picture – a picture of Father, Son, and Holy Spirit existing simultaneously.

The Bible even shows the three persons of the Godhead as eternally distinct. The Father and Son love one another, speak to each other, and together send the Holy Spirit. Additionally, Jesus proclaims that He and the Father are two distinct witnesses and two distinct judges (John 8:14-18).

Such self-distinctions are amplified through the announcement of Christ's birth (Luke 1:35), His baptism (Luke 3:22), and His commission to baptize believers "in the name of the Father and of the Son and of the Holy Spirit" (Matt. 28:19).

A LATE INVENTION?

Some critics of the Trinity doctrine protest that it is a late invention, formulated only after the Roman Emperor Constantine, a convert to Christianity, decreed an end to all persecution of Christians in AD 313 and convened the first ecumenical council at Nicaea in AD 325. But the charge of doctrinal invention simply isn't true, as we see from Scripture and the history of early Christians, who embraced both the deity of Christ and the deity and personhood of the Holy Spirit – although admittedly they often struggled to understand the mystery behind it.

Yes, the councils of Nicaea and Constantinople (AD 381) produced the Nicene Creed, but neither the councils nor Constantine manufactured the Trinity. Rather, the Nicene Creed settled the question of how Christians can worship one God and also claim that God is three persons. It was also the first creed (a formal statement of Christian beliefs) to obtain universal authority in the church, and it improved the language of the Apostles' Creed by including more specific statements about the deity of Christ and the Holy Spirit.[11]

As Millard Erickson points out, there is no virtue in continuing to hold such a difficult doctrine as the Trinity if it is not actually taught in the Bible: "The church ... drew the inference of the Trinity from two sets of evidence it accepted. On the one hand, the Bible taught that God is one. On the other hand, there were three persons whom the Bible seemed to identify as being divine."[12]

While the councils articulated the doctrine of the Trinity, they did not invent it. Rather, they sought to counter a creeping heresy that an Alexandrian presbyter named Arius spread early in the fourth century. Arius proclaimed his theory that Jesus was not God. Instead, He was only a celestial servant of the true Most High God, who alone was almighty, transcendent, the Creator and first cause of all things. Jesus, therefore, was a lesser being, highly exalted but created – a view that Jehovah's Witnesses champion today.

After years of vigorous debate, the councils produced the Nicene Creed as a way of articulating what Scripture teaches about the nature and persons of the Godhead. The final form reads, in part:

> I believe in one God, the Father Almighty, Maker of heaven and earth, and of all things visible and invisible.
>
> And in one Lord Jesus Christ, the only-begotten Son of God, begotten of the Father before all worlds; God of God, Light of Light, very God of very God; begotten, not made, being of one substance with the Father, by whom all things were made ...
>
> And I believe in the Holy Ghost, the Lord and Giver of Life; who proceeds from the Father and the Son; who with the Father and the Son together is worshipped and glorified; who spoke by the prophets ...[13]

As Nathan Jacobs observes, "In the most basic sense, then, Nicene Trinitarianism affirms that the Father, Son, and Holy Spirit are three distinct individuals or subjects who share a common nature, namely, the nature of God. This is what it means to confess the Holy Trinity as three *hypostases* of one *ousia*."[14]

The Greek word *ousia* refers to the nature or essence of something. For example, let's say Bob, Judy, and Cybil are in the room. The *ousia* of these three is human. That's the nature these three persons share. But with respect to *hypostasis*, this word depicts an individual or a particular subject. In other words, Bob, Judy, and Cybil are three persons – *hypostases* – who share one *ousia*: humanity.

Put simply, there is only one divine nature, and only three persons share it: Father, Son, and Holy Spirit. While Scripture indicates that followers of Jesus share the divine nature (2 Pet. 1:4), it does not mean we become gods or absorb the immutable qualities of the Godhead, such as omniscience. Rather, it means the Holy Spirit brings life to our human spirits and makes us more like Jesus as we submit to the will of God (2 Pet. 1:4-11).

HOW THE BIBLE USES THE WORD "GOD"

To avoid confusion, we need to understand three different ways the Bible employs the word "God" and the way we use it in our theology. Otherwise, we may be tempted to see the Trinity as three gods.

First, there are references to God as *Father*. The New Testament often uses this approach to distinguish between God the Father and Jesus. For example, 1 Corinthians 8:6 reads, "… yet for us there is one God, the Father. All things are from him, and we exist for him. And there is one Lord, Jesus Christ. All things are through him, and we exist through him."

Paul further writes in 2 Corinthians 1:3, "Blessed be the God and Father of our Lord Jesus Christ, the Father of mercies and the God of all comfort."

Second, there are references to the *divine nature* that the Father, Son, and Holy Spirit share. For example, John writes, "and the Word was with God, and the Word was God" (John 1:1). This does not mean that Jesus (here called "the Word") is the Father. Rather, it means Jesus and the Father share the divine nature. Further, the Holy Spirit is called the Spirit of God and the Spirit of Christ (Rom. 8:9; 1 Pet. 1:11).

This was important to early church leaders, for it helped distinguish belief in the Trinity from polytheism. Polytheists believed in many species of god – or many divine beings –

while Christianity was adamant in its defense of true worship of one God – that is, one divine nature expressed in three persons.

Third, the word "God" is a reference to the entire Trinity. This usage of the term is a later development in Christianity, but it's no less true. When Genesis 1:1 states, "In the beginning, God created the heavens and the earth," we come to understand by reading additional Scriptures that the Father, Son, and Holy Spirit are involved in the creation of all things (Gen. 1:1-2; John 1:3; Col. 1:15).

As we close this chapter, we would do well to remember a few key biblical truths about the Trinity. First, God is spirit. So, we should avoid thinking of the Father, Son, and Holy Spirit as three separate bodies. All creatures are finite and, with the exception of angels, material. But God alone is both infinite and immaterial. The three persons of the Godhead, therefore, do not have separate bodies, as Bob, Judy, and Cybil have. Jesus, of course, took on a body in the Incarnation, but He did not lay aside His deity. Thus, He never broke eternal fellowship with the Father and the Holy Spirit.

Second, the persons of the Godhead are distinguished by name. There is the Father. He is the Father because He begets the Son. What makes the Son the Son is that He is begotten by the Father. What makes the Holy Spirit the Holy Spirit is that He is the "breathed one." The English word "spirit" in Greek and Hebrew also means "wind" or "breath." Put another way, the Spirit communicates the holy presence of the transcendent God.

As the Nicene Creed points out, the Father receives divinity from no one; He is unbegotten. But the Son and the Holy Spirit receive their divinity from the Father. This does not mean they are created, or that they came into existence sometime after the Father, for the Nicene Creed speaks of the Son as "begotten of the Father before all worlds." Drawing on language from Scriptures such as Proverbs 8:23, John 17:5, and Colossians 1:15, we may speak of the Son as begotten from eternity. The Father has begotten the Son from eternity, and the Spirit has eternally proceeded from the Father and the Son.

While this is difficult to grasp, it's important because it distinguishes a biblically faithful understanding of the Trinity from false concepts of the Godhead, as well as from denials of it. Nathan Jacobs puts this in perspective: "We might think of it like the relationship between the sun and its rays and heat. If the sun were eternal, then its rays and heat would be eternal also. But the rays and heat would still be caused by the sun: they would be eternally generated. So, the Father eternally begets the Son and spirates the Spirit. He never began doing so."[15]

Third, the members of the Trinity are not autonomous. They never existed apart from each other. There was never a time when Jesus did not exist as the Son of God. Neither was there a time when the Holy Spirit did not exist as the Breathed One. As eternally existing persons, Jesus was always the Son of God, and the Holy Spirit was always the Spirit of God.

The persons of the Trinity, therefore, may be distinguished but never separated.[16]

REVIEW

1. While it's true that the word _____ is not found in English Bible translations, that doesn't mean the doctrine is missing in action. Scripture describes God as one eternal _____ in three persons: Father, Son, and Holy Spirit.

2. It may help our understanding of the Trinity to distinguish between *being* and *person*. Your *being* is the quality that makes

you _____ you are. Your *person* is the quality that makes you _____ you are. In a sense, then, God is one "what" (being) and three "whos" (persons).

3. With respect to the doctrine of the Trinity, the Bible teaches three simple truths:

(a) There is only _____ true God.

(b) The Father is God; the _____ is God; and the Holy Spirit is _____.

(c) The Father, Son, and Holy Spirit are _____, but inseparable, persons who _____ simultaneously.

4. Some critics of the Trinity doctrine protest that it is a late _____, formulated only after the Roman Emperor _____, a convert to Christianity, decreed an end to all persecution of Christians in AD 313 and convened the first ecumenical council at _____ in AD 325. But Scripture and early church history show that first-century Christians embraced both the _____ of Christ and the deity and _____ of the Holy Spirit.

5. To avoid confusion, we should understand three different ways the Bible employs the word "God" and the way we use it in our theology:

(a) There are references to God as _____.

(b) There are references to the _____ nature that the Father, Son, and Holy Spirit share.

(c) The word "God" often is a reference to the entire
_____.

THINK

Questions for personal or group study

1. Imagine you are visiting with a Jehovah's Witness, who shares her conviction that your belief in the Trinity is false. She points to your Bible and says, "Show me where I can find the word Trinity in there." How would you respond?

2. Why is it important to distinguish between God as one *being* in three *persons*?

3. Our Muslim friends may argue that we should reject the doctrine of the Trinity because it's too complicated, or even self-contradicting. After all, they say, how can one equal three? How might you answer that charge?

4. What are some ways people misunderstand, or even mischaracterize, the doctrine of the Trinity?

5. Why were the councils of Nicaea and Constantinople important to the doctrine of the Trinity? Do councils establish Christian doctrines? Or is their role to faithfully understand, articulate, and apply them?

The church has consistently taught that the Father, Son, and Holy Spirit are three persons in that each is aware of the others, speaks to the others, and loves and honors the others while sharing divine attributes such as omniscience, omnipotence, and omnipresence.

CHAPTER TWO

False Views of the Trinity

As we pursue a biblically faithful understanding of the Trinity, it may help to sort through a number of false views of this crucial doctrine. Some of these faulty definitions are grounded in misunderstanding, such as the Muslim view that Christians are polytheists for worshiping God, Jesus, and Mary.[1] Others are subtler in that they properly identify the persons of the Godhead yet reduce the Father, Son, and Holy Spirit to pieces of a divine puzzle, or as three separate gods. So, as we briefly explore these flawed depictions of the Trinity, it's important to keep in mind that the Bible reveals one true and living God, who exists as three distinct, but inseparable, co-equal, co-eternal persons – Father, Son, and Holy Spirit.

TRITHEISM

Tritheism is the teaching that the Godhead essentially consists of three separate gods. While it is accurate to say the Father is God, the Son is God, and the Holy Spirit is God, it is wrong to say that these three persons constitute three separate deities. Recall that in Chapter One we distinguished between *being* and *person*. God is one being. At the same time, the Father,

Son, and Holy Spirit are distinct, but inseparable, persons who share the divine nature.

Tritheism has taken different forms throughout church history. One ancient view was that the divine nature is divided into three parts, analogous to a lump of clay cut into three pieces.[2] In the late eleventh century, Roscelin, a Catholic monk in France, considered the three divine persons as three independent beings who, it could be said, were three gods. Roscelin maintained that God the Father and God the Holy Spirit would have become incarnate with God the Son unless they maintained their separate identities as three gods.[3]

In contrast, the church has consistently taught that the Father, Son, and Holy Spirit are three persons in that each is aware of the others, speaks to the others, and loves and honors the others while sharing divine attributes such as omniscience, omnipotence, and omnipresence. The three persons who share these "omni" attributes are in effect one being, not three separate beings. For example, if the Father knows everything, so do the Son and the Holy Spirit. Their shared knowledge of all things demonstrates their oneness of being, even though they may be distinguished as persons.

UNITARIANISM

Unitarianism takes many forms, but essentially it maintains that God is only one divine person (the Father) and denies that Jesus Christ is God in that sense. Historically, the term has been used in reference to Socinianism – a form of non-trinitarianism that emerged around the same time as the Protestant Reformation, holding the view that Jesus was merely human – and to modern forms of Arianism such as Jehovah's Witness theology.[4]

James White, in *The Forgotten Trinity*, writes that many Christians, without knowing it, hold a false view of the Trinity due to their inability to articulate the difference between believing in one *being* of God and three *persons* sharing that one being. As a result, they unwittingly slip into an ancient error known today as Oneness, or the 'Jesus Only' position.[5]

The Oneness doctrine accepts the truth that there is only one true God, but it explains this to mean that the Father, Son, and Holy Spirit are all titles for Jesus Christ. Oneness denies that the Bible differentiates between the three as real persons. Instead, advocates of this position either believe the Father is the Son, and the Son is the Spirit, and the Spirit is the Father – like an actor on a stage wearing different masks to play different parts – or they make the Son merely the "human nature" of Christ (hence denying His eternal nature). Jesus then either becomes, in effect, two "persons," the Father and the Son, or the Father is equated with His divine nature and the Son with His human nature.

Here are some brief definitions of various terms referring to Unitarianism:

Modalism – the belief that there is one God in substance and person, and that the Father, Son, and Holy Spirit are three successive functions, or modes, of that God but not distinct persons. In Old Testament times, God appeared as the Father. At the Incarnation, He showed up as the Son. And after Jesus' ascension, He manifested Himself as the Holy Spirit. Modalism teaches that these modes are consecutive and never simultaneous. Put another way, this view argues that the Father, Son, and Holy Spirit never exist at the same time – only one after the other. Modalism denies the distinctiveness of the persons of the Godhead, although it retains the deity of Christ.[6]

Sabellianism – another way of viewing the modalistic view of God. Sabellius, a third-century priest, argued that God is like an actor wearing several masks – first, the mask of the

Father, then the mask of the Son, and finally the mask of the Holy Spirit. But behind these masks is just one person.[7]

Patripassianism – the seemingly logical consequence of modalism that if there is no real distinction between the Father and the Son, then the Father must have suffered on the cross.

Oneness Pentecostalism – a modern anti-Trinitarian sect that denies any distinctions among the persons of the Godhead. Jesus is God, but He also is the Father and the Holy Spirit. In a slight deviation from ancient modalism, Oneness Pentecostals teach that God is able to manifest Himself in all three "modes" simultaneously, such as at Jesus' baptism (Luke 3:22).[9]

POLYTHEISM

Polytheism is the belief that there are multiple deities. Followers of Judaism, Islam, and a number of counterfeit forms of Christianity often accuse orthodox Christians of being polytheists. They say we worship three Gods: Father, Son, and Holy Spirit. This, of course, is a serious misunderstanding of the Trinity. Christians insist that the one true God exists in tri-unity or "threeness" – that is, three distinct persons but only one essence or being.

Polytheism is both ancient and enduring. The Egyptians believed in Ra, Osiris, Amun, Isis, and other deities. The Greeks worshiped Zeus, Poseidon, Aphrodite, Artemis, and more. The Romans assimilated much of Greek polytheistic culture while adding a few gods of their own, such as Janus. In addition, Romans worshiped spirits and engaged in the deification of their emperors.[10]

Over time, polytheism spread in Asian, African, and European cultures, emerging in such religions as Hinduism,

Mahayana Buddhism, Taoism, and Shintoism.[11] The Church of Jesus Christ of Latter-day Saints is polytheistic, teaching that deified men rule their own kingdoms throughout the universe and that human beings are gods in embryo. They profess the Father, Son, and Holy Ghost as three separate gods. It may be more accurate to depict Latter-day Saints as *henotheists*. While they acknowledge the multiplicity of gods, they insist that "Heavenly Father" (*Elohim*, or the god of this world) is the only god with which they are concerned.

This is not to say that all religions rejecting polytheism are the same. Christian monotheism is distinct from the monotheism of Judaism and Islam. While we agree with Jews and Muslims that there is only one divine nature, and that polytheism is wrong to profess many deities, Judaism and Islam are anti-Trinitarian in their monotheism. Islam, in fact, declares that anyone professing the belief in Jesus as the Son of God commits the unpardonable sin, known as *shirk*.

As Nathan Jacobs makes clear, "It should be obvious, however, that those who affirm the Trinity disagree with those who deny the Trinity. If your understanding of God is no different than that of someone who rejects the Trinity, you're not a Trinitarian. Christians are monotheists. But more fundamentally, Christians are Trinitarians. This monotheism is unique."[12]

HENOTHEISM

While not strictly a false concept of the Trinity, henotheism is something of a hybrid between polytheism and monotheism. A henotheist is committed to one god, while leaving room for other deities. As R. C. Sproul explains it, "Henotheism is belief in one god ... but the idea is that there is one god for each people or nation, and each one reigns over a particular geographical area. For example, henotheism would hold that there was a god for the Jewish people (Yahweh), a god for the

Philistines (Dagon), a god for the Canaanites (Baal), and so on. However, this view does not posit that there was only one god ultimately."[13]

Hinduism, although polytheistic, may be offered as an example of henotheism. Hindus generally worship one god, yet they acknowledge more than three hundred million other gods who may be worshiped as well. Ancient Egyptians believed in many gods, but at times they elevated one above the others. And the religion of the ancient Greeks venerated the Olympians, with Zeus as the supreme ruler of the others.[14]

Perhaps the best modern-day example of henotheism comes from the Church of Jesus Christ of Latter-day Saints. The church professes belief in the Trinity, although it describes both the Father and the Son as deities of flesh and bone, with the Holy Ghost a divine "personage of spirit."[15] In addition, the church acknowledges the existence of countless other gods who rule over equally countless universes. Yet Latter-day Saints are called to focus their attention on Heavenly Father. As one of the church's teaching tools puts it, "We shouldn't forget that God is literally our Father in Heaven," meaning he produced all people in the pre-mortal spirit realm through sexual relations with a goddess wife.[16]

These and other errant doctrines should lead us to conclude that the LDS Church is not the true church, as it claims, and that henotheism, while common throughout history, does not properly capture the nature of the one true God.

THE FAILURE OF ANALOGIES

In seeking to simplify the complex truth of one God in three persons, Christians sometimes resort to analogies. An analogy is a comparison between two things for the purpose of explanation or clarification. While analogies applied to the Trinity seem helpful on the surface, they fail to do justice to our infinite and eternal God. Worse, according to Nathan Jacobs, "each represents an ancient heresy."[17]

As Jacobs points out, Trinitarian analogies typically fall into three groups:

Parts-whole. In parts-whole analogies, the Trinity may be likened to an egg, which has a shell, egg white, and egg yolk. Each part is fully egg but not the whole egg, and thus each part is distinct from one another. As another example, the Trinity sometimes is said to be like a three-leaf clover. Each leaf is distinct from the others, but the clover is incomplete without all three. One other example, from ancient times, is that the Trinity is like a single lump of clay divided into three parts.

Parts-whole analogies are similar to the heresy of Tritheism, which we discussed earlier in this chapter. Tritheism takes on two basic forms: (1) the belief that the Father, Son, and Holy Spirit are three separate divine beings, and (2) that the divine nature may be divided into three parts, like the shell, egg white, and egg yolk, or like a lump of clay cut into three pieces.[18] This reduces God to the sum of His parts.

Names. The second set of analogies applies several names to one subject. For example, one man can be a father, a son, and a husband. This analogy comes close to the ancient heresy of Sabellianism. Earlier, we learned Sabellius taught that God is like an actor wearing several masks, one each depicting the Father, Son, and Holy Spirit, but with one person (God) behind them.[19]

States. The third group of analogies identifies a single substance that may take on different states. H_2O, for instance, is one compound that may be a solid, a liquid, or a gas.[20] However, this suggests that the divine nature is like a substratum that produces several distinct persons – a view that Basil of Caesarea, a third-century Trinitarian, called blasphemous.[21]

While it's true that a quantity of H_2O may be converted to a liquid, solid, or gas, and then converted to another state, God does not swap persons within the Godhead; the Father never becomes the Son, for example. This view inadvertently mirrors modalism.

So, perhaps it's best for us to stick with the simple truths we laid out in the first chapter: There is one God. This one divine being exists as three distinct, but inseparable, co-equal, co-eternal persons – Father, Son, and Holy Spirit. These three persons always have existed in a loving relationship, and together they created the universe and carried out a plan to redeem lost sinners and restore them to a right relationship with the triune God.

While the existence of God as one being in three persons is mysterious, why would we expect God to be any simpler than His creation? Many biblical truths are mysterious or, at the very least, difficult to understand. The virgin birth of Jesus, for example, is a miracle that has never been replicated. How the eternal Son of God added sinless humanity to His deity via His conception in Mary's womb through the work of the Holy Spirit is mind-boggling, to say the least. Yet, that's the way the Son of God condescended to become like fallen people in order to win us back, satisfying the wrath of God and extending to us His grace and mercy.

The doctrine of divine election is equally challenging. How is it that a sovereign God chooses certain individuals for salvation and, at the same time, endows all human beings with an ability to make choices for which they are held accountable? The biblical truths of God's sovereignty and human responsibility are indisputable. And yet they have sparked more than a few vigorous debates over the centuries.

It is perhaps best for us to take God at His word, to understand as much as we are able, and then to go no further by trying to reconcile what God has revealed as a mystery. After all, as Yahweh declares in Isaiah 55:8-9: "'For my thoughts are not your thoughts, and your ways are not my ways.' This is the Lord's declaration. 'For as heaven is higher than earth, so my ways are higher than your ways, and my thoughts than your thoughts.'"

REVIEW

1. Some faulty views of the Trinity are grounded in misunderstanding. For example, Muslims call Christians polytheists who worship God, Jesus, and _____. Other misunderstandings are subtler in that they properly identify the _____ of the Godhead yet reduce the Father, Son, and Holy Spirit to pieces of a divine _____, or as three separate gods.

2. Tritheism has taken different forms throughout church history. One ancient view was that the divine _____ is divided into three parts, like a lump of clay cut into three pieces. Another view, which arose in the eleventh century, considered the three divine persons as three _____ beings, and thus as three distinct _____.

3. Unitarianism takes many forms, but essentially it maintains that God is only one divine _____ (the Father) and denies that Jesus Christ is God in that sense. Historically, the term has been used in reference to Socinianism, and to modern forms of _____ such as Jehovah's Witness theology. Different expressions of Unitarianism include:

(a) Modalism – the belief that the Father, Son, and Spirit are three successive _____, or modes, of God who appear consecutively but never simultaneously.

(b) Sabellianism – the view that God is like an _____ wearing several masks.

(c) Patripassianism – the seemingly logical consequence of modalism that if there is no real _____ between the Father and the Son, then the Father must have suffered on the _____.

(d) Oneness Pentecostalism – a modern anti-Trinitarian sect that denies any _____ among the persons of the Godhead.

4. Polytheism is the belief that there are _____ deities. Polytheism is both ancient and enduring. The Egyptians, _____, and Romans all worshiped a pantheon of gods. In addition, the Romans worshiped spirits and engaged in the deification of their _____. A hybrid form of polytheism and monotheism is known as _____.

5. In seeking to simplify the complex truth of the Trinity, Christians sometimes resort to _____, which are comparisons of two things for the purpose of explanation or clarification. While these comparisons seem helpful on the surface, they fail to do justice to God. Worse, they inadvertently represent ancient _____.

THINK

Questions for personal or group study

1. You find yourself visiting with a Muslim, who regards all Christians as polytheists for worshiping three divine beings: God, Jesus, and Mary. Knowing that the Qur'an – Islam's most holy book – teaches this erroneous view of the Trinity,

how might you begin to respectfully address this misunderstanding?

2. What are two different forms of Tritheism? And how do these false views of the Trinity fail to properly distinguish between *being* and *person* with respect to God?

3. A popular anti-Trinitarian sect today is Oneness Pentecostalism. What do Oneness Pentecostals believe about the Father, Son, and Holy Spirit? Why are these beliefs unbiblical?

4. Jews, Muslims, and Christians all claim to be monotheists; that is, we believe there is only one true God. What distinguishes Christian monotheism from that of Judaism and Islam?

5. We've all heard analogies designed to help us understand the complex nature of the Trinity: God is like an egg with three parts – shell, egg yolk, and egg white; God is like a person who is a father, a son, and a husband all at the same time; God is like H_2O, which can be solid, liquid, or gas. Why do these analogies fail to do justice to our triune God? And which ancient heresies do these analogies resemble?

While many belief systems — from Islam to the Watch Tower — profess monotheism, they fail to project a biblically faithful doctrine of the oneness of God.

CHAPTER THREE

One God

The Bible consistently declares that there is only one true and living God, the self-revealed Creator who alone must be loved and worshiped. All other gods are false. The physical depictions of these gods, as carved images or naturally occurring phenomena such as stars and trees, in fact represent demons.

In the Song of Moses, the leader of Israel declares, "They provoked his [Yahweh's] jealousy with different gods; they enraged him with detestable practices. They sacrificed to demons, not God, to gods they had not known, new gods that had just arrived, which your fathers did not fear" (Deut. 32:16-17). Using synonymous parallelism, in which two or more lines communicate the same idea using different words, Moses makes it clear that "different gods" are in fact "demons." Grammatically, the demons and the foreign gods are the same.[1]

The apostle Paul picks up the same theme as he warns the Corinthians against idolatry: "What am I saying then? That food sacrificed to idols is anything, or that an idol is anything? No, but I do say that what they sacrifice, they sacrifice to demons and not to God. I do not want you to be participants with demons!" (1 Cor. 10:19-20). To Christians, an idol is nothing (1 Cor. 8:4). That is, while demons may tempt, harass, and seek to influence our behavior, they have no final authority over us. Even so, we must be aware that Satan desires to be worshiped (Matt. 4:9) and that demons teach false doctrines in order to deceive people (1 Tim. 4:1).

THE SHEMA

Perhaps nowhere is the exclusivity of God stated more clearly than in the *Shema*, an affirmation of Judaism and a declaration of faith in one God. It is the oldest fixed daily prayer in Judaism, recited morning and night since ancient times.[2] It consists of three biblical passages, two of which instruct the Israelites to speak of these things "when you lie down and when you rise up." This is fulfilled by including the *Shema* in the liturgy for the *Ma'ariv* (evening services) and *Shacharit* (morning services). Traditional prayer books also include a *Bedtime Shema*, a series of passages including the *Shema* to be read at home before turning in for the evening.

Perhaps the best-known part of the *Shema* is from the first biblical passage: "Listen, Israel: The Lord our God, the Lord is one. Love the Lord your God with all your heart, with all your soul, and with all your strength" (Deut. 6:4-5).[3]

The prophet Isaiah echoes this cry as he calls the Israelites to return to the Lord. Isaiah 44:6 – 45:25 is a powerful reminder from Yahweh that He alone is God. Consider just a portion of this passage:

> "This is what the Lord, the King of Israel and its
> Redeemer, the Lord of Armies, says:
> I am the first and I am the last.
> There is no God but me" (44:6).
>
> "Is there any God but me?

There is no other Rock; I do not know any" (44:8).

"This is what the Lord, your Redeemer who formed
 you from the womb, says:
 I am the Lord, who made everything;
 who stretched out the heavens by myself; who
 alone spread out the earth" (44:24).

"I am the Lord, and there is no other;
 there is no God but me" (45:5).

"I made the earth,
 and created humans on it.
 It was my hands that stretched out the heavens,
 and I commanded everything in them" (45:12).

"For this is what the Lord says —
 the Creator of the heavens,
 the God who formed the earth and made it,
 the one who established it
 (he did not create it to be a wasteland,
 but formed it to be inhabited) —
 he says, 'I am the Lord,
 and there is no other'" (45:18).

"Turn to me and be saved,
 all the ends of the earth.
 For I am God,
 and there is no other" (45:22).

The Lord even injects humor into His self-defense, mocking the idol makers:

"The woodworker stretches out a measuring line,
 he outlines it with a stylus;

  he shapes it with chisels
  and outlines it with a compass.
  He makes it according to a human form,
  like a beautiful person,
  to dwell in a temple.

He cuts down cedars for his use,
  or he takes a cypress or an oak.
  He lets it grow strong among the trees of the forest.
  He plants a laurel, and the rain makes it grow.

A person can use it for fuel.
  He takes some of it and warms himself;
  also he kindles a fire and bakes bread;
  he even makes it into a god and worships it;
  he makes an idol from it and bows down to it.

He burns half of it in a fire,
  and he roasts meat on that half.
  He eats the roast and is satisfied.
  He warms himself and says, 'Ah!
  I am warm, I see the blaze.'

He makes a god or his idol with the rest of it.
  He bows down to it and worships;
  he prays to it, 'Save me, for you are my god.'

Such people do not comprehend
  and cannot understand,
  for he has shut their eyes so they cannot see,
  and their minds so they cannot understand.

No one comes to his senses;
  no one has the perception or insight to say,
  'I burned half of it in the fire,

>   I also baked bread on its coals,
>   I roasted meat and ate.
>   Should I make something detestable with the rest of it?
>   Should I bow down to a block of wood?'
>
> He feeds on ashes.
>   His deceived mind has led him astray,
>   and he cannot rescue himself,
>   or say, 'Isn't there a lie in my right hand?'" (44:13-20)

CONTINUITY IN COVENANTS

The New Testament consistently upholds the theme of one God:

Mark 12:29-30 – In response to a scribe who asks about the greatest commandment, Jesus replies, "The most important is Listen, O Israel! The Lord our God, the Lord is one. Love the Lord your God with all your heart, with all your soul, with all your mind, and with all your strength."

1 Corinthians 8:4-6 – In response to a question about food offered to idols, Paul writes, "About eating food sacrificed to idols, then, we know that 'an idol is nothing in the world,' and that 'there is no God but one.' For even if there are so-called gods, whether in heaven or on earth — as there are many 'gods' and many 'lords' — yet for us there is one God, the Father. All things are from him, and we exist for him. And there is one Lord, Jesus Christ. All things are through him, and we exist through him."

Ephesians 4:4-6 – Paul writes, "There is one body and one Spirit — just as you were called to one hope at your calling — one Lord, one faith, one baptism, one God and Father of all, who is above all and through all and in all."

1 Timothy 2:5-6 – Paul again writes, "For there is one God and one mediator between God and humanity, the man

Christ Jesus, who gave himself as a ransom for all, a testimony at the proper time."

While the theme of one God runs consistently through Scripture, both the Old and New Testaments offer us increasing light into the existence of this one being in three persons – a topic we explore in future chapters.

J. I. Packer writes that the basic assertion of the doctrine of the Trinity is that the unity of the one God is complex. "The three personal 'substances' (as they are called) are coequal and coeternal centers of self-awareness, each being 'I' in relation to two who are 'you' and each partaking of the full divine essence (the 'stuff' of deity, if we may dare to call it that) along with the other two."[4]

ONE IN MANY WAYS

Not only is Yahweh one God, but the Bible depicts Him as unique. That is, God is one of a kind in a number of ways:

First, Yahweh is the only true God, standing apart from the false gods of the pagan world.

Jeremiah 10:10 – "But the Lord is the true God; he is the living God and eternal King. The earth quakes at his wrath, and the nations cannot endure his rage."

John 17:3 – "This is eternal life: that they may know you, the only true God, and the one you have sent – Jesus Christ."

1 Thessalonians 1:9 – "… for they themselves report what kind of reception we had from you: how you turned to God from idols to serve the living and true God …"

Second, Yahweh is the only eternal God. All idols fashioned with human hands, and every demon behind them, had a beginning and will have an end (in judgment).

Genesis 21:33 – "Abraham planted a tamarisk tree in Beer-sheba, and there he called on the name of the Lord, the Everlasting God."

Isaiah 40:28 – "Do you not know? Have you not heard?

The Lord is the everlasting God, the Creator of the whole earth. He never becomes faint or weary; there is no limit to his understanding."

Romans 16:26 – "… but now revealed and made known through the prophetic Scriptures, according to the command of the eternal God to advance the obedience of faith among all the Gentiles …"

Third, Yahweh is the only living God. Unlike lifeless, graven idols, the Lord has life in Himself and is eternally self-existent (John 5:26).

1 Samuel 17:26 – Speaking of Goliath, David asks his fellow Israelites, "Just who is this uncircumcised Philistine that he should defy the armies of the living God?"

Daniel 6:26 – King Darius declares, "I issue a decree that in all my royal dominion, people must tremble in fear before the God of Daniel: For he is the living God, and he endures forever; his kingdom will never be destroyed, and his dominion has no end."

Acts 14:15 – When Paul and Barnabas are mistaken for gods in Lystra, Paul rushes into the crowd and shouts, "People! Why are you doing these things? We are people also, just like you, and we are proclaiming good news to you, that you turn from these worthless things to the living God, who made the heaven, the earth, the sea, and everything in them."

Fourth, Yahweh is the only God by nature. While other gods compete for our attention, whether the "god of this age" (2 Cor. 4:4) or the god of our own appetites (Phil. 3:19), only Yahweh is divine in essence.

Romans 1:25 – Describing the depravity of the Gentile world, Paul writes, "They exchanged the truth of God for a lie, and worshiped and served what has been created instead of the Creator, who is praised forever. Amen."

1 Corinthians 10:20-21 – In warning against idolatry, Paul declares, "… what they [idolaters] sacrifice, they sacrifice to demons and not to God. I do not want you to be participants with demons! You cannot drink the cup of the Lord and the cup of demons. You cannot share in the Lord's table and the table of demons."

Galatians 4:8 – "But in the past, since you didn't know God, you were enslaved to things [or beings] that by nature are not gods."

Fifth, Yahweh is the only Creator. Some forms of counterfeit Christianity ascribe creation to a "council of gods" or even to Jesus as a created being through whom Jehovah created all other things. But the Bible is clear that Yahweh alone is the maker of heaven and earth.

Isaiah 37:16 – "Lord of Armies, God of Israel, enthroned between the cherubim, you are God – you alone – of all the kingdoms of the earth. You made the heavens and the earth."

Isaiah 44:24 – "This is what the Lord, your Redeemer who formed you from the womb, says: I am the Lord, who made everything; who stretched out the heavens by myself; who alone spread out the earth …"

Jeremiah 10:10-12, 16 – "But the Lord is the true God; he is the living God and eternal King. The earth quakes at his wrath, and the nations cannot endure his rage. You are to say this to them: 'The gods that did not make the heavens and the earth will perish from the earth and from under these heavens.' He made the earth by his power, established the world by his wisdom, and spread out the heavens by his understanding…. He is the one who formed all things."[5]

HEBREW SCRIPTURES AND THE TRINITY

While most arguments for the Trinity are grounded in the New Testament, God begins revealing His triune nature in the Old Testament. One hint at the plurality and unity of the Godhead may be found in several passages where God speaks.

For example, Genesis 1:26 reads, "Then God said, 'Let us

make man in our image, according to our likeness.'" Here, the verb "said" is singular, but the verb "let us" is plural, as are the possessive endings of the nouns "our image" and "our likeness." Then, in the next verse we read, "So God created man in his own image; he created him in the image of God; he created them male and female" (v. 27).

Genesis 3:22-24 provides a similar clue: "The Lord God said, 'Since the man has become like one of *us*, knowing good and evil, he must not reach out, take from the tree of life, eat, and live forever.' So the Lord God sent him away from the garden of Eden to work the ground from which he was taken. *He* drove the man out ..." (emphasis added).

Other examples include:

- Genesis 11:7, where the Lord says, "Come, *let's* go down there and confuse their languages so that they will not understand one another's speech." Then, in verses 8 and 9, *the Lord* "scattered them" and "confused the language of the whole earth" (emphasis added).
- Isaiah 6:8 – "Then I heard the voice of the Lord asking: Who should *I* send? Who will go for *us*?" (emphasis added).

Commentators provide a variety of explanations for these verses. Some contend that, in the Genesis passages, God is addressing a council of heavenly creatures entrusted with authority on earth. These creatures would include cherubim, who we encounter in Genesis, Ezekiel, and elsewhere, as guardians of God's holiness (Gen. 3:24; Exod. 36:35; 1 Kings 6:23-29; Ezek. 1:5-26; 10:1-22). In the Isaiah 6 passage, Yahweh may be speaking to a heavenly court that includes the seraphim, six-winged creatures that stand above God's throne and declare His holiness (see verses 2-3, 6-7).

Others scholars assert that these texts show the Lord

speaking to subordinates He used in the process of creation. Still others say Yahweh is employing the "plural of majesty" used of important people, like kings; its plural form does not necessarily designate any sort of plurality. And then, some ancient writings and commentaries simply alter or delete these passages.[6]

While we should take note of these Old Testament texts, we don't want to press the issue too strongly, since God's self-revelation in Scripture is progressive. As we move through the Old Testament and into the New Testament, we see more clearly the revealed truth of one God in three persons.

Before moving on, we should note there are crucial differences in the ways the world's three major monotheistic religions – Judaism, Islam, and Christianity – understand the reality of one God. Judaism holds strongly to the doctrine of one God and rejects the Christian doctrine of the Trinity. Yet, ancient Israelites taught that the Hebrew Bible bore witness to two Yahweh figures – "two powers" in heaven, one invisible and the other visible, the visible power being the Angel of the Lord.[7]

Islam also denies the Trinity, embracing a monolithic oneness in its concept of God. The Muslim doctrine of *tawhid* declares that Allah is absolutely and singularly one. He takes no "partners." That is, he acknowledges no other divine members of a godhead. He is not relational, which means human beings cannot be considered his sons and daughters. Allah reveals his will, not himself. To say that Jesus is the Son of God is to commit the unpardonable sin of *shirk*, which damns a soul to hell.

Some Muslim theologians go so far as to argue that because Allah is a *monad* – an indivisible and hence ultimately simple entity – he cannot have eternal attributes like compassion and mercy, for they would curb his absolute unity. In other words, Allah expresses compassion only after creating objects of compassion, such as human beings; love is what he *does*, not who he *is*.[8]

In contrast, the God of the Bible is triune: one being in three persons. Father, Son, and Holy Spirit are eternally loving and relational. Their attributes, such as love and mercy, are not contingent on creation, for these divine traits are eternal and unchanging. Further, Yahweh creates people with a Godlike capacity for personality, selfless love, and relationships with one another and, more importantly, with their Creator.

OTHER GODS

In Scripture, the Hebrew word *elohim* is used thousands of times for the singular God of Israel, but not exclusively. The biblical writers also employ *elohim* to refer to members of God's heavenly host, lesser divine beings in Yahweh's heavenly council or assembly (Ps. 89:5-7); gods and goddesses of nations surrounding Israel (Judg. 11:24; 1 Kings 11:33); territorial spirits (Hebrew: *shedim*, often translated "demons," Deut. 32:17); and the spirits of deceased people (1 Sam. 28:13).[9] As Michael Heiser notes, "A biblical writer would use *elohim* to label any entity that is not embodied by nature and is a member of the spiritual realm."[10]

In every case, these other "gods" are created beings, none of whom shares the unique qualities of Yahweh (omnipotence, omniscience, omnipresence, transcendence, immutability, etc.). They owe their existence, power, knowledge, and authority to Yahweh and ultimately are accountable to Him. So, when Scripture states there is no God but Yahweh, and also speaks of other gods, we should not see this as a contradiction. Rather, we should see it as a way the biblical writers describe the residents of the spiritual realm.

Every member of the spiritual world may be thought of as *elohim* since the term tells us where an entity belongs with respect to its nature. Heiser explains, "The spiritual realm has rank and hierarchy: Yahweh is the Most High. Biblical writers distinguish Yahweh from other *elohim* by means of other descriptors exclusively attributed to him, not by means of the single word *elohim*."[11] But we should keep in mind that there is only one Yahweh. As the prophet Nehemiah explicitly states, "You, Lord, are the only God" (Neh. 9:6).

This idea carries through into the New Testament. 1 Corinthians 8:5-6 is helpful, as the apostle Paul writes, "For even if there are so-called gods, whether in heaven or on earth – as there are many 'gods' (*theoi*) and many 'lords' (*kurioi*) – yet for us there is one God, the Father. All things are from him, and we exist for him. And there is one Lord, Jesus Christ. All things are through him, and we exist through him." Paul's theology is in line with Old Testament writers who affirm multiple *elohim* but only one Yahweh. Writing to believers in a city infested with false deities, Paul refers to these same "gods" and "lords" in 1 Corinthians 10:19-22, calling them "demons."

As we've already seen, Judaism and Islam profess belief in one God but depart from Christianity's view of God as triune. In a similar manner, many counterfeit forms of Christianity also profess belief in one God, but they, too, define Him unbiblically.

Members of the Church of Jesus Christ of Latter-day Saints concern themselves primarily with Elohim, or Heavenly Father, who once was a man and progressed to divine status. Latter-day Saints also profess belief in the Trinity, which founder Joseph Smith defined as three separate gods. Heavenly Father and Jesus have physical bodies of flesh and bone, while the Holy Ghost is a non-physical god who inhabits the spirit realm. But it doesn't stop there. Latter-day Saints pursue personal "exaltation," or godhood, themselves, following the example of Heavenly Father. In effect, Latter-day Saints are henotheists. That is, they acknowledge many gods but focus their worship on one particular god.

Jehovah's Witnesses are staunch defenders of monotheism, but they perpetuate the Arian heresy of the fourth century, viewing Jesus as a lesser, created divine being. More to the point, they believe Jehovah stands alone as God; that Jesus is the first being Jehovah created (as Michael the Archangel); and that "holy spirit" is an impersonal force Jehovah uses to accomplish His will on earth. Jehovah's Witnesses are so hostile to the doctrine of the Trinity that their leaders in the Watch Tower Bible and Tract Society once wrote, "The clergy's God is plainly not Jehovah but the ancient deity, hoary with the iniquity of the ages – Baal, the Devil Himself."[12]

Oneness Pentecostals profess belief in one God as well. However, they believe God is a single person, manifesting Himself successively as Father, Son, and Holy Spirit. This view mirrors the ancient heresy of Monarchianism.

All of the above-mentioned belief systems profess monotheism. Yet none of them projects a biblically faithful doctrine of the oneness of God, which is essential to a proper understanding of the persons of the Trinity – our focus in the next chapter.

REVIEW

1. The Bible consistently declares that there is one — and only one — true and living God, the self-revealed _____ who alone must be loved and worshiped. All other gods are _____, and the physical depictions of these gods, as carved images or naturally occurring things, in fact represent _____.

2. Perhaps nowhere is the doctrine of one God stated more clearly than in the _____, an affirmation of Judaism and a declaration of faith in one God. It is the oldest

fixed daily prayer in _____, recited morning and night since ancient times.

3. Isaiah 44:6 – 45:25 is a powerful reminder from _____ that He alone is God. Verse 6 of Isaiah 44 reads: "This is what the Lord, the King of Israel and its Redeemer, the Lord of Armies, says: I am the _____ and I am the _____. There is no _____ but me."

4. The New Testament consistently _____ the theme of one true and living God. In 1 Timothy 2:5-6, the apostle Paul writes, "For there is one _____ and one _____ between God and humanity, the man Christ Jesus, who gave himself as a ransom for all, a testimony at the proper time."

5. In Scripture, the Hebrew word _____ is used thousands of times for the singular _____ of Israel, but not exclusively.

THINK

Questions for personal or group study

1. The Bible acknowledges the existence of many gods. What distinguishes these gods from Yahweh, the one true and living God?

2. What is the *Shema*, and why is it still important to Jews and Christians today?

3. Read Isaiah 44:6 – 45:25. How many times, and in what different ways, does Yahweh declare Himself the only God? In what ways does God mock those who fashion and worship gods of metal and wood?

4. What are some different ways the Hebrew word *elohim* is used in the Bible? How is *elohim* different from the name *Yahweh*?

5. Besides biblical Christianity, what are some other belief systems that claim to worship the one true God? How are their gods different from Yahweh? Specifically, think of Islam, The Church of Jesus Christ of Latter-day Saints, and the Watch Tower Bible and Tract Society.

If only the Father is eternal, and the Son and Holy Spirit are brought into existence, then who did the Father love when He was all alone?

CHAPTER FOUR

Three Persons

The Bible is clear that there is one true God. And yet, three distinct persons make up the Godhead: Father, Son, and Holy Spirit. How is this possible? Or, as some critics pose the question, how can one equal three?

The key to solving this quandary, as we discussed in Chapter One, is to distinguish between *being* and *person*. God is one *being* who is eternal, all-powerful, all-knowing, and everywhere present. At the same time, three *persons* share these unique, transcendent qualities. Put another way, God is one *what* and three *whos*. When we say God is a Trinity, we are describing the *what* of God. When we speak of the Father, Son, and Holy Spirit, we are referring to the *who* of God – three persons, indivisible in essence but distinct in identity.

The three persons of the Godhead perform different roles. Yet they are united in purpose. Consider the so-called "Eternal Covenant of Redemption." In eternity past, the Father, Son, and Holy Spirit voluntarily and freely chose the roles they would take in securing our redemption. The Father chose to be the source of salvation. The Son chose to be the Savior who became a man (without surrendering His deity) and submitted to the Father's will. The Spirit chose to bear testimony of Jesus and to be the indwelling presence of Yahweh in the hearts of believers.

As James White summarizes, *"difference in function does not indicate inferiority of nature.* That is, just because the Father, Son, and Spirit *do* different things does not mean that any one of them is *inferior* to the others in *nature."* He goes on to say that many arguments against the deity of Christ and the Trinity make one major false assumption: "that for either the Son or the Spirit to be truly and fully God, *they have to do the exact same things as the Father in the exact same way."*[1]

The truth, however, is that different roles in redemption do not make any of the divine persons of the Godhead inferior or superior to the others. The same is true of the Trinity's work of creation. While Scripture often depicts Jesus as the agent of creation, and the Father as creation's source, it does not logically follow that the Son is a lesser being. Quite the contrary. Jesus shares all the attributes of deity with the Father, including eternality (John 8:58), authority (Matt. 28:18), equality (John 10:30), and form (Phil. 2:6). Similarly, the Father and the Son send the Holy Spirit, but this does not render them superior to the Comforter who came in power on the Day of Pentecost.

OUR RELATIONAL GOD

When we speak of God as Father, Son, and Holy Spirit, we acknowledge not only the distinctions between the three persons of the Godhead, but the eternal relationships they share. Yahweh is relational. The persons of the Trinity did not develop intimacy with one another over time; they always existed in loving, selfless relationships that set the standard for our relationships with God as well as with one another.

The apostle John depicts Jesus as living from all eternity in "the bosom of the Father" (John 1:18 NASB), an ancient metaphor for love and intimacy. Later in John's Gospel, Jesus describes the Spirit as living to "glorify" Him (John 16:14). At the same time, the Son glorifies the Father (John 17:4) and the Father glorifies the Son (John 17:5).

What does the term "glorify" mean? Tim Keller explains, "To glorify something or someone is to praise, enjoy, and delight in them.... To glorify someone is also to serve or defer to him or her. Instead of sacrificing their interests to make yourself happy, you sacrifice your interests to make them happy. Why? Your ultimate joy is to see them in joy."[2] What this means for the Trinity, then, is that each person loves, adores, defers to, and rejoices in the others.

Cornelius Plantinga writes, "The Father ... Son ... and Holy Spirit glorify each other.... At the center of the universe, self-giving love is the dynamic currency of the Trinitarian life of God. The persons within God exalt, commune with, and defer to one another.... When early Greek Christians spoke of *perichoresis* in God they meant that each divine person harbors the others at the center of his being. In constant movement of overture and acceptance each person envelops and encircles the others."[3]

So, *perichoresis* is eternal – as timeless as Yahweh. Think about the phrase, "God is love," for a moment. The Bible teaches this truth (1 John 4:8), and we accept it without question. But John's statement has profound implications regarding the nature of Yahweh. God's love (Greek: *agape*) is more than a fleeting emotion (*eros*), or even an enduring friendship (*phileo*). It is inextricably tied to the eternality of the triune God.

If only the Father is eternal, and the Son and Holy Spirit are brought into existence, then who did the Father love when He was all alone? He could only choose to love the Son and the Holy Spirit *after* they arrived. In this case, God could not be described as a being who *is*, by nature, love, only someone who expresses love toward finite beings as an act of divine will. But if the three persons of the Godhead are eternal, so is their love for one another. Then it rightly may be said, "God is love."

Contrast this scintillating truth about Yahweh's nature with the nature of Allah, the god of Islam. The Qur'an depicts him as merciful, compassionate, and forgiving. But these terms describe what Allah *does*, not who he *is*. Allah is monolithic, completely separate from everything and everyone. He does not take "partners" – that is, divine or human sons or daughters. For Muslims, to suggest that Jesus is the Son of God, or that God exists as a Trinity, is reprehensible. For Allah to love someone or something, he must first create objects worthy of love. Therefore, in stark opposition to Yahweh, Allah is not a lover by nature.

The triune God of the Bible, however, has always loved because it is God's eternal nature to do so. The Father, Son, and Holy Spirit have always loved one another. This eternal love is showered on human beings – not as a result of creating objects of love, but as an overflow of divine, eternal love that permeates the very being of God. Put another way, God is a community of persons who have loved each other for all eternity. And God designed us to join that community as adopted sons and daughters.

The apostle Paul writes, "For all those led by God's Spirit are God's sons. You did not receive a spirit of slavery to fall back into fear. Instead, you received the Spirit of adoption, by whom we cry out, '*Abba*, Father!' The Spirit himself testifies together with our spirit that we are God's children, and if children, also heirs – heirs of God and coheirs with Christ – if indeed we suffer with him so that we may also be glorified with him" (Rom. 8:14-17).

Take a moment and breathe in that reality. The Holy Spirit leads all of God's children, who have been born again and adopted into the family of God. The indwelling Spirit does more than passively reside in our human spirits. He places God's mark of ownership on us through sealing. He plunges us into the universal church through Spirit baptism. He sets us apart and works continually to conform us to the image of Christ in sanctification. He empowers us to serve by granting us spiritual gifts. He helps us understand the book He authored as we read it and meditate on its inspired passages. He whispers comfort, encouragement, and correction into our spiritual ears so that we might hear His voice over the white noise of fleshly appeals.

What's more, Paul writes that we should not despair about the slavery of fear, from which Christ has delivered us. Rather, we should rest in the reality of everlasting life, which the "Spirit of adoption" has secured for us. In that warm glow of unbreakable familial love, we may call God *Abba* – our Papa.

Then, the Spirit testifies with our spirits that we are children of God. Even more, we are coheirs with Christ. The certainty of Jesus' role as the heir of all things should remind us of His words, "I will not leave you as orphans; I am coming to you.... Because I live, you will live too" (John 14:18-19). We should celebrate the distinct personhood and common purpose of each member of the Godhead.

The ultimate reason God creates is not to compensate for some shortcoming within the Godhead – loneliness, for example – but to extend the triune God's perfect bond of intimacy to human beings created to be Yahweh's imagers.

As one writer puts it, "God's joy and happiness and delight in divine perfections is expressed externally by communicating that happiness and delight to created beings.... The universe is an explosion of God's glory. Perfect goodness, beauty, and love radiate from God and draw creatures to ever increasingly share in the Godhead's joy and delight.... The ultimate end of creation, then, is union in love between God and loving creatures."[4]

PERSONHOOD IN PRACTICE

Let's briefly consider just a few ways in which the personhood of the Father, Son, and Holy Spirit is expressed in Scripture.

The Father

Robert Morey writes, "The concept of God the Father was revealed in the earliest books of the Old Testament and slowly reached its full meaning in the New Testament. But its development from the bud to the flower does not negate its existence."[5] The Bible reveals the Father as divine; His deity is clearly depicted and unrivaled in the pages of Scripture. At the same time, He is intimately personal. For example, God the Father is:

- The Father of Israel: "Yet Lord, you are our Father; we are the clay, and you are our potter; we all are the work of your hands" (Isa. 64:8; see also Exod. 4:22-23; Deut. 14:1; Jer. 31:9).
- The Father of the Messiah: "You are my Son; today I have become your Father" (Ps. 2:7; see also Prov. 30:4).
- The Father of Christians: "See what great love the Father has given us that we should be called God's children – and we are!" (1 John 3:1; see also John 1:12).

God the Father displays personal attributes. To name a few, He is:

- Love: "And we have come to know and to believe the love that God has for us. God is love, and the one who remains in love remains in God, and God remains in him" (1 John 4:16).

- Gracious: "He did not even spare his own Son but offered him up for us all. How will he not also with him grant us everything?" (Rom. 8:32).
- Made known through the Son: "No one has ever seen God. The one and only Son, who is himself God and is at the Father's side – he has revealed him" (John 1:18).
- Merciful: Jesus tells His followers, "Be merciful, just as your Father also is merciful" (Luke 6:36).

In the New Testament alone, there are more than three hundred references to the Father. He knows (Matt. 6:8); speaks (Matt. 3:17); sees (Matt. 6:4); loves (1 John 3:1); wills (Matt. 7:21); gives or does not give (Matt. 7:11); reveals or hides (Matt. 11:25); is or is not pleased (Mark 1:11); forgives or does not forgive (Matt. 6:14-15); sends (1 John 4:14); and much more. These are the activities of a person and, as such, there should be no doubt about the personhood of God the Father.

The Son

Jesus of Nazareth is a real historical person. At the same time, He is unique in that His conception in Mary's virgin womb is not the beginning of His existence. The Bible reveals Jesus as the eternal Son of God. His deity and personhood extend from eternity past to eternity future. In becoming a man, Jesus adds sinless humanity to His deity, yet He does not become a different person. Throughout Scripture, we see Jesus exhibiting the qualities of personhood.

In the Old Testament, we see several appearances by the Angel (or Messenger) of Yahweh. As Michael Heiser explains, "This figure is actually Yahweh himself in the visible form of a man. Consequently, the angel of Yahweh is central to the concept of a Godhead.... This concept is at the heart of the ancient Jewish teaching that the Hebrew Bible bore witness to two Yahweh figures — 'two powers' in heaven, one invisible and the other visible."[6] More about this Messenger in Chapter Six. We also see Jesus depicted as the Son of Man on the clouds of heaven, approaching the Ancient of Days (Dan. 7:13); Wonderful Counselor, Mighty God, Eternal Father, and Prince of Peace (Isa. 9:6); and the one whose "origin is from antiquity, from ancient times" (Mic. 5:2).

When we come to the New Testament, we see more clearly that Jesus is an eternal, divine person:

- He is the Word who created all things (John 1:1-3).
- He becomes flesh – that is, He adds sinless humanity to His deity (John 1:14).
- He exists before Abraham as the eternal I AM (John 8:58).
- He shares the glory of the Father before the world exists (John 17:5).
- He is equal with God the Father (John 10:30; Phil. 2:6).
- He is the radiance of God's glory and the exact expression of God's nature (Heb. 1:3).
- He is the First and the Last, the Living One (Rev. 1:17).

In His earthly ministry, Jesus exhibits all the qualities of human and divine personhood: He knows (John 2:24); speaks (Matt. 5:1); sees (John 1:48); loves (Mark 10:21); wills (Matt. 26:39); gives or does not give (John 17:2); reveals or hides (Matt. 11:27); is pleased (2 Cor. 5:9); forgives (Mark 2:5); sends (John 20:21); dies (1 Cor. 15:3); and much more. The human authors of Scripture use "He," "Him," and "His" to point to the personhood of the Messiah.

Just as 1 John 1:3 illustrates the personhood of the Father, it also invites us to intimacy with the Son: "[W]hat we have seen and heard we also declare to you, so that you may also have fellowship with us; and indeed our fellowship is with the Father and with his Son Jesus Christ."

THE HOLY SPIRIT

The Holy Spirit sometimes is relegated to an inferior, supporting role when it comes to discussions of the Trinity. Worse, in some forms of counterfeit Christianity, His deity and personhood are denied. Jehovah's Witnesses, for example, describe "holy spirit" as God's "active force," an impersonal force likened to electricity. This is more than unfortunate; it is without support in Scripture. The Bible clearly reveals the Holy Spirit as both divine and personal.

In the Old Testament, the Spirit of God hovers over the waters and is active in the creation of all things, giving us an early indication of the deity and personhood of the Spirit (Gen. 1:2). When the children of Israel rebel against God, they grieve the Holy Spirit; only a person may be grieved (Isa. 63:10). The prophet Micah asks, "Is the Spirit of the Lord impatient?" (Mic. 2:7). This reveals that ancient Jews believed the Spirit was a person capable of becoming annoyed with their sins. King David testifies on his death bed, "The Spirit of the Lord spoke through me, his word was on my tongue" (2 Sam. 23:2).

There's more. The Spirit gives wisdom, knowledge, understanding, and artistic abilities to people (Exod. 31:3; Isa. 11:2); He informs judges (Judg. 3:10); and He motivates God's people to prayer (Zech. 12:10). Other Old Testament examples could be cited, but these illustrate the truth that the Holy Spirit is both divine and personal – a truth that carries forward into the New Testament. Consider:

- The Spirit convicts unbelievers of sin, Christ's righteousness, and judgment (John 16:7-11).

- Followers of Jesus have fellowship with the Holy Spirit (2 Cor. 13:13).
- The Spirit ensures our adoption as children of God (Rom. 8:14-17).
- The Holy Spirit may be lied to, and grieved (Acts 5:3; Eph. 4:30).

In addition, the Holy Spirit hears (John 16:13); searches everything (1 Cor. 2:10); speaks (Mark 13:11); testifies (John 15:26); counsels (John 16:7); guides (John 16:13); glorifies Christ (John 16:14); declares (John 16:14); forbids (Acts 16:6-7); intercedes (Rom. 8:26); separates and sends out people (Acts 13:1-4); sets elders over the church (Acts 20:28); distributes spiritual gifts (1 Cor. 12:11); and much more.

DISTINCT, NOT SEPARATE

While the three persons of the Godhead are distinct, they cannot be separated. That is, the Father, Son, and Holy Spirit are co-equal and co-eternal. They exist simultaneously, not consecutively. Let's summarize this essential truth, drawing from Scripture:

- The Father, Son, and Holy Spirit are present together at Jesus' baptism (Matt. 3:13-17; Mark 1:9-11; Luke 3:21-23).
- In the Great Commission, Jesus sends His followers to make disciples in "the name [singular] of the Father and of the Son and of the Holy Spirit ..." (Matt. 28:19-20).
- The three persons of the Godhead work together to grant spiritual gifts to Jesus' followers: "Now there are different gifts, but the same Spirit. There are different ministries, but the same Lord [Jesus]. And there are different activities, but the same God

[Father] produces each gift in each person. A manifestation of the Spirit is given to each person for the common good" (1 Cor. 12:4-7).
- The members of the Trinity are engaged together in the sealing of Christ's followers: "Now it is God [the Father] who strengthens us together with you in Christ, and who has anointed us. He has also put his seal on us and given us the Spirit in our hearts as a down payment" (2 Cor. 1:21-22).
- Paul closes his second letter to the Corinthians with a Trinitarian benediction: "The grace of the Lord Jesus Christ, and the love of God, and the fellowship of the Holy Spirit be with you all" (2 Cor. 13:13).
- The Father, Son, and Holy Spirit cooperate for our salvation: "When the time came to completion, God [the Father] sent his Son, born of a woman, born under the law, to redeem those under the law, so that we might receive adoption as sons. And because you are sons, God [the Father] sent the Spirit of his Son into our hearts, crying, '*Abba*, Father!'" (Gal. 4:4-6).
- Christian unity is centered on the Trinity: "There is one body and one Spirit – just as you were called to one hope at your calling – one Lord [Jesus], one faith, one baptism, one God and Father of all, who is above all and through all and in all" (Eph. 4:4-6).
- The three persons of the Godhead perform complementary works of salvation: "To those chosen ... according to the foreknowledge of God the Father, through the sanctifying work of the Spirit, to be obedient and to be sprinkled with the blood of Jesus Christ" (1 Pet. 1:1-2).
- The Father, Son, and Spirit are involved in the resurrection that secures our salvation: "For Christ

also suffered for sins once for all, the righteous for the unrighteous, that he might bring you to God [the Father]. He was put to death in the flesh but made alive by the Spirit ..." (1 Pet. 3:18).

While additional Trinitarian passages could be cited, the passages above offer abundant evidence that the three persons of the Godhead are divine, personal, co-equal, and co-eternal.

A TRINITARIAN MATRIX

In *Reordering the Trinity,* Rodrick Durst catalogues a treasure trove of Trinitarian references in the New Testament – seventy-five in all. Every one of the six possible groupings – Father-Son-Spirit; Father-Spirit-Son; Son-Father-Spirit; Son-Spirit-Father; Spirit-Son-Father; Spirit-Father-Son – appears multiple times in nineteen of the twenty-seven New Testament books. James is the only New Testament author whose writings do not feature at least one Trinitarian reference.

Durst writes, "My research shows that the quantity of divine triadic instances is so profound and in such diversity of orders that it constitutes a qualitative *matrix* of Trinitarian consciousness. Trinity is how the New Testament authors inadvertently thought and viewed reality.... such a profound and generous distribution of triadic references demonstrates that the Trinitarian way of praying, communing, thinking, and teaching was a part of Christianity from its start."[7]

That is not to say the Old Testament offers no evidence of a Trinitarian matrix. Church leaders as early as Tertullian, at the beginning of the third century, wrestled with the Old Testament's way of revealing diversity within the oneness of Yahweh. For example, in Genesis 1:1-3 we see *Elohim* (God) creating, with the Spirit (*ruach*) hovering until God speaks, and with His Word creation comes into being.

Other examples:

Isaiah 11:1-3 – A Branch from the roots of Jesse will bear fruit; the Spirit of the Lord will rest on Him; and His delight will be in the fear of the Lord. This Messianic passage distinguishes the Branch (Messiah), the Spirit, and the Lord, yet all three act in unity of purpose.

Isaiah 42:1 – The Lord, speaking in the first person, and identified later as God, introduces "my servant; I strengthen him, this is my chosen one; I delight in him. I have put my Spirit on him …" So, we see the Lord, the servant (Messiah), and the Spirit, yet this passage strongly affirms monotheism in verse 8: "I am the Lord. That is my name, and I will not give my glory to another or my praise to idols."

Isaiah 48:16 – Here, the Servant speaks in the first person: "Approach me and listen to this. From the beginning I have not spoken in secret; from the time anything existed, I was there. And now the Lord God has sent me and his Spirit."

Isaiah 61:1 – The Messiah speaks: "The Spirit of the Lord God is on me, because the Lord has anointed me to bring good news to the poor …" Some seven hundred years later, Jesus inserts Himself into this very triad when He reads this text in a Nazarene synagogue service and then says, "Today as you listen, this Scripture has been fulfilled" (Luke 4:21).

Ezekiel 37 – In Ezekiel's vision of the valley of the dry bones, we encounter the Lord, the Spirit, and the Word. To achieve His purposes of restoration and reunification among His people, the Lord (Father) uses His Spirit and His Word.

These threefold ways of differentiating the presence of Yahweh throughout the Old Testament are not explicit proofs of the Trinity. Yet, as Durst concludes, they "constitute a theological mode of thought for Jesus and the writers of the New Testament."[8]

In conclusion, as we read through Scripture, it becomes evident that the Father, Son, and Holy Spirit are divine, personal, and eternally relational. As we see in coming chapters, the deity and personality of the three persons of the Godhead, while challenging to comprehend, are truths all Christians should embrace. These truths give us more than a picture of Yahweh; they provide comfort, strength, and hope as we walk the path of good works God paved for us in eternity past (Eph. 2:10). Though we must navigate a sinful and fallen world, the triune God promises to one day set things right.

REVIEW

1. The three persons of the Godhead perform different roles. Yet they are united in _____. In the "Eternal Covenant of Redemption," the Father chose to be the _____ of salvation. The Son chose to be the _____ who became a man (without surrendering His deity), and the Holy Spirit chose to bear testimony of Jesus and to be the _____ presence of Yahweh in the hearts of believers.

2. When we speak of God as Father, Son, and Holy Spirit, we acknowledge, not only the distinctions between the three persons of the Godhead, but the eternal _____ they share. The persons of the Trinity always have existed in loving, _____ relationships that set the standard for our relationships with God and one another.

3. The triune God of the Bible always has loved because it is God's eternal _____ to do so. The Father, Son, and Holy Spirit have always loved one another. This eternal love is showered on human beings – not as a result of creating _____ of love, but as an overflow of divine, eternal love that permeates the very being of God.

4. The ultimate reason God creates is not to _____ for some shortcoming within the Godhead – loneliness, for example – but to extend the triune God's perfect bond of _____ to human beings created to be Yahweh's imagers.

5. The Holy Spirit sometimes is relegated to an inferior, supporting role when it comes to discussions of the Trinity. Worse, in some forms of _____ Christianity, His deity and personhood are denied. Jehovah's Witnesses, for example, describe "holy spirit" as God's "active _____," an impersonal force likened to _____. Yet the Bible clearly reveals the Spirit as both _____ and personal.

THINK

Questions for personal or group study

1. Think about the different roles of the Godhead in salvation. What does the Father do? What does the Son do? And what does the Holy Spirit do? How would you respond to the critic who says that because the Father, Son, and Holy Spirit play different roles, they can't all be truly and fully God?

2. What does the term "glorify" mean? How does it apply to the relationship between the persons of the Godhead? And how does it set an example for us in our relationship with Jesus Christ?

3. The Qur'an depicts Allah as merciful, compassionate, and forgiving. But these terms describe what Allah *does*, not who he *is*. Since Allah is monolithic, having no "partners," he must first create objects worthy of mercy, compassion, or forgive-

ness in order to extend these actions to them. How is this different from the God of the Bible?

4. Read Romans 8:14-17. What roles do the Father, Son, and Holy Spirit play in God's saving work of adoption? How do these roles illustrate the personhood of each member of the Godhead?

5. Scripture clearly reveals the personhood of the Father, Son, and Holy Spirit. What do the following Bible passages say about this:

The Father

John 1:18 – He is revealed in the person of _____.
Rom. 8:32 – He did not even spare His own _____.
1 John 3:1 – He has given us such great love that we are called His _____.
1 John 4:16 – He is _____.

The Son

John 1:1-3 – He is the Word who _____ all things.
John 1:14 – He became _____, adding sinless humanity to His deity.
John 8:58 – He existed before _____ as the eternal I AM.
John 10:30; Phil. 2:6 – He is _____ with God the Father.

The Holy Spirit

Genesis 1:2 – He _____ over the waters and was active in creation.

John 16:7-11 – He convicts unbelievers of sin, Christ's righteousness, and _____.
Acts 5:3; Eph. 4:30 – He may be lied to, and _____.
2 Corinthians 13:13 – He gives followers of Jesus _____ with Him.

Distinct but inseparable persons

Matthew 28:19-20 - In the Great Commission, Jesus sends His followers to make disciples in the _____ of the Father, Son, and Holy Spirit.
Ephesians 4:4-6 - Christian unity is centered on the Trinity. There is one body and one _____ , one Lord [Jesus], one faith, one baptism, one God and _____ of all.
1 Peter 1:1-2 – Believers are _____ according to the foreknowledge of God the Father, through the sanctifying work of the _____, to be obedient and to be sprinkled with the blood of Jesus Christ.
1 Peter 3:18 - The Father, Son, and Spirit are involved in the _____ that secures our salvation.

"Only the Trinitarian can truly worship God the Father because only the Trinitarian worships the Son and the Holy Spirit."

— Robert Morey

CHAPTER FIVE

The Father is God

There is little dispute among professing Christians that our Heavenly Father is God. This is true even among the most prominent forms of counterfeit Christianity. Jehovah's Witnesses, for example, believe in the deity and personhood of Jehovah, whom they identify as the Father, even though they deny the doctrine of the Trinity and embrace unbiblical views about Jesus and the Holy Spirit. Members of the Church of Jesus Christ of Latter-day Saints profess belief in Heavenly Father, or *Elohim*, whom they worship as the god of this world, although he is one of a multitude of gods and potential gods.

These doctrinal distinctions highlight the importance of defending historic Christianity. If we fail to understand the Father correctly, and if we miss the clear teachings of Scripture with respect to His relationship with the other members of the Godhead, then the biblical doctrines of creation, redemption, and restoration suffer as well.

As Robert Morey writes, "The notion that all religions worship the Father just under different names is an idea totally foreign and antithetical to the Bible. Only the Trinitarian can truly worship God the Father because only the Trinitarian worships the Son and the Holy Spirit."[1]

Just as it is possible to preach "another Jesus ... a different spirit ... a different gospel" (2 Cor. 11:4), it likewise is possible to preach another Father. Islam actually denies the fatherhood of God, depicting Allah as singular, monolithic, non-relational, and unknowable. Latter-day Saints worship a Heavenly Father who once was a mortal man with his own Father who was God before him. Further, they believe that Heavenly Father and a heavenly Mother are our literal parents in heaven. Since Jehovah's Witnesses believe Jesus is a created being, they cannot worship God as the eternal Father. And the Father worshiped in the United Pentecostal Church is not the Father of Scripture since they believe Jesus *is* the Father.

In this chapter, we examine the deity of the Father (we discussed His personhood in Chapter Four), and then we see how the fatherhood of God is revealed in His relationship with the Son, with Israel, and with the church. Along the way, we come to understand that while the Father's deity is shared with Jesus and the Holy Spirit, He extends to us, as sinful and fallen creatures, an everlasting relationship with Him as His adopted children.

THE DEITY OF THE FATHER

It's important to note while the Father is a person, He is not human. First, the Bible explicitly denies that the Father is a man. The Old Testament prophet Balaam – a scoundrel who prophesied for hire – nevertheless spoke the truth concerning God's unchanging decrees when he said, "God is not a man, that he might lie, or a son of man, that he might change his mind. Does he speak and not act, or promise and not fulfill?" (Num. 23:19).

On another occasion, the prophet Samuel informs Saul that the Lord has torn away the kingship of Israel from Saul and given it to David. "Furthermore," he says, "the Eternal one of Israel does not lie or change his mind, for he is not man who changes his mind" (1 Sam. 15:29). Other Old Testament passages make similar claims (Job 9:32; Isa. 31:3; Hosea 11:9).

In the New Testament, when Peter declares Jesus the Christ, the Son of the living God, Jesus says to the disciple, "Blessed are you, Simon son of Jonah, because flesh and blood did not reveal this to you, but my Father in heaven" (Matt. 16:17). No human being revealed the truth to Peter. It was the Father in heaven.

Not only does the Bible clearly deny the humanity of the Father; it affirms His divine, eternal nature as spirit. Jesus tells the Samaritan woman at the well that "an hour is coming, and is now here, when the true worshipers will worship the Father in Spirit and in truth. Yes, the Father wants such people to worship him. God is spirit, and those who worship him must worship in Spirit and in truth" (John 4:23-24).

When the Bible tells us that no one has seen God, it is a reference to the Father, who is spirit (John 1:18; 4:24). The apostle Paul declares that Jesus is "the image of the invisible God" (Col. 1:15). The writer of Hebrews describes Jesus as "the radiance [or reflection] of God's glory and the exact expression of his nature" (Heb. 1:3). Jesus puts it more plainly when He tells Philip, "The one who has seen me has seen the Father" (John 14:9).

To summarize: The Father is a divine, eternal, non-human person who is immortal and invisible.

THE FATHERHOOD OF GOD

Now, let's look at some ways the Bible describes the Father as God:

The Greek word *theos* is used of the Father. We see this in numerous passages, such as Galatians 1:1; Philippians

2:11; 1 Peter 1:2; 2 John 1:3; and Jude 1. While *theos* also is used of Satan (2 Cor. 4:4) and pagan idols (1 Cor. 8:5), the New Testament writers are clear that these entities are not God by nature (Gal. 4:8). In fact, Paul argues that the gods of the pagans actually are demons (1 Cor. 10:20).

In addition, the Greek *kyrios* (Lord) is found more than seven hundred times in the New Testament and is clearly applied to the Father in numerous passages (Matt. 4:7; 5:33; 11:25; 21:9; Mark 12:36; Acts 4:26; 7:49; 2 Cor. 6:18; Heb. 12:5-6).

While it's true that *kyrios* sometimes is used in the New Testament as a term of respect – as in "sir" – and does not automatically imply deity, the New Testament writers often employ *kyrios* when referring to God in quotations from the Old Testament. To cite but one example, Psalm 118:26 says, "He who comes in the name of the Lord [Yahweh] is blessed …" The New Testament writers quote this passage numerous times, using *kyrios*, thus affirming the deity of the Father (Matt. 21:9; 23:39; Mark 11:9; Luke 13:35; 19:38; John 12:13).

The Father's divine attributes reveal His deity. The Father is eternal (Rom. 1:20; 16:26; 1 Tim. 6:16); almighty (Rev. 19:6); immortal (1 Tim. 1:17); all-knowing (Matt. 6:32); perfect (Matt. 5:48); and true deity (John 17:3).

We should not overlook the significance of 1 John 1:3, where the apostle writes, "[W]hat we have seen and heard we also declare to you, so that you may also have fellowship with us; and indeed our fellowship is with the Father and with his Son Jesus Christ." The invitation to fellowship with the Father, as with the Son, demonstrates both His personhood and His deity.

The Father performs the works of God. These include creation (Heb. 2:10); sovereignty (Matt. 11:25); providence (Matt. 5:45; 6:26); the authority to judge (John 5:22; Rom. 14:10-12); the bestowing of life (John 5:21, 26); and salvation (Eph. 1:4).

In John 5, after Jesus heals a disabled man, the Jewish leaders begin persecuting Jesus because He performs this miracle on the Sabbath. In response, Jesus calls God His Father, making Himself equal with God (v. 18). Further, He describes the divine authority the Father has given Him for His earthly ministry. This authority includes working (vv. 17, 19); revealing Himself (v. 20); raising the dead (v. 21); judging (vv. 22, 27); receiving honor (v. 23); granting eternal life (vv. 24-26); resurrecting all people (vv. 28-29); and revealing His divine will (v. 30).

The Father speaks the words of God. In Romans 1, Paul claims he is called as an apostle and set apart for the gospel of God, which He [the Father] promised beforehand through His prophets in the Holy Scriptures, concerning His Son, Jesus Christ (vv. 1-3). And in Hebrews 1, the writer declares, "Long ago God spoke to the fathers by the prophets at different times and in different ways. In these last days, he has spoken to us by his Son …" (vv. 1-2).

The Father is worshiped as God. Scripture often directs us to worship the Father. We are to "ascribe to the Lord the glory due his name; worship the Lord in the splendor of his holiness" (Ps. 29:2); "worship and bow down" (Ps. 95:6); "go to his dwelling place … worship at his footstool" (Ps. 132:7); "worship the Father in Spirit and in truth" (John 4:23); "be grateful for receiving a kingdom that cannot be shaken, and thus let us offer to God acceptable worship, with reverence and awe" (Heb. 12:28 ESV).[2]

Jesus declares the Fatherhood of God. For Jesus, "God" and "Heavenly Father" are synonymous expressions. Jesus clearly has the Father in mind in many references to God. On the cross, in a prayer of agony to the Father, He cries, "My God, my God, why have you abandoned me?" (Matt. 27:46). This shout of anguish, as Jesus bears our sin debt, comes between other prayers of intimacy with the Father. As He is nailed to the cross and hoisted between two criminals, Jesus prays, "Father, forgive them, because they do not know what they are doing" (Luke 23:34). Then, just before He breathes His last, Jesus shouts, "Father, into your hands I entrust my spirit" (Luke 23:46).

In Matthew 6:26-30, Jesus uses "God" and "Father" interchangeably. He assures His followers of divine care, noting that "your heavenly Father feeds" the birds (v. 26) and "God clothes the grass of the field" (v. 30). Then, in verses 31-32, Jesus states that we shouldn't worry about food, drink, and clothing because "your heavenly Father knows that you need them."

The Bible reveals God as the Father of all humanity. Last, we should note that Scripture shows Yahweh to be the Father of all people through creation. Humans are fashioned in God's image, so to the extent that we are His creatures, He is our Father. Paul exclaims to the Athenians on Mars Hill, "For in him we live and move and have our being, as even some of your own poets have said, 'For we are also his offspring.' Since we are God's offspring then, we shouldn't think that the divine nature is like gold or silver or stone, an image fashioned by human art and imagination" (Acts 17:28-29).

In his instructions to the Corinthians about eating food offered to idols, Paul writes, "yet for us there is one God, the Father. All things are from him, and we exist for him" (1 Cor. 8:6). To the Ephesians, as Paul addresses unity and diversity in the body of Christ, he notes that there is "one God and Father of all, who is above all and through all and in all" (Eph. 4:6). And James tells his readers, "Every good and perfect gift is from above, coming down from the Father of lights, who does not change like shifting shadows" (James 1:17).

The fatherhood of God in relation to all people should not be confused with His special relationships with His Son, with Israel, and with followers of Jesus, as we are about to see.

THE GOD AND FATHER OF OUR LORD JESUS CHRIST

While Jesus assures His followers that God is their Heavenly Father, He alone shares a unique relationship with the Father as the eternal Son of God. There is an intimacy in this union that only exists between two eternal, all-powerful, and all-knowing persons. We explore this relationship in more detail in the next two chapters. Still, it may prove helpful here to note a few New Testament passages where Paul and Peter use the phrase "the God and Father of our Lord Jesus Christ." How is it that Yahweh is both the God of Jesus, and His Father?

Let's begin with the verses themselves, and then follow up with a few observations.

Romans 15:6 – "so that you may glorify the God and Father of our Lord Jesus Christ with one mind and one voice."

2 Corinthians 1:3 – "Blessed be the God and Father of our Lord Jesus Christ, the Father of mercies and the God of all comfort."

Ephesians 1:3 – "Blessed is the God and Father of our Lord Jesus Christ, who has blessed us with every spiritual blessing in the heavens in Christ."

1 Peter 1:3 – "Blessed be the God and Father of our Lord Jesus Christ. Because of his great mercy he has given us new birth into a living hope through the resurrection of Jesus Christ from the dead."

To understand how Yahweh is both the God of Jesus and His Father, we need to keep in mind the triune nature of God. The one true God exists as three distinct, but inseparable, co-equal, co-eternal persons. About Jesus, consider:

- Like the Father, Jesus is eternal and uncreated (John 1:1).

- Jesus shared the Father's glory before the world existed (John 17:5).
- Jesus, like the Father and the Holy Spirit, is the Creator of all (John 1:3; Col. 1:16-17).
- However, Jesus is unique in that He added sinless humanity to His deity through the miracle of the virgin birth. Thus, Jesus retained His deity, even when becoming flesh and dwelling among us (John 1:14).

As the second person of the Godhead, Jesus freely refers to God as His Father – a relationship they always have shared. In Chapter Twelve, we see how the word "Son" perhaps best refers to likeness rather than inferiority. As the co-equal second person of the Trinity, Jesus is deity revealed in the flesh (John 1:1, 14; Col. 2:9). Jesus never *becomes* the Son of God; He *is*, eternally, the Son. Passages such as Hebrews 1:5 – "You are my Son; today I have become your Father" (quoting Ps. 2:7) – should be understood in context as referring to the resurrection and exaltation of Jesus. We examine more closely Jesus as "begotten" in Chapter Six.

In His humanity, Jesus comes as our Savior. He must live a fully human life in order to be our substitute. He is born under the law (Gal. 4:4), which means He is obligated to love God and honor Him (Deut. 6:4-5). So Jesus has to obey the law, which He does, even though He is tempted in every way we are tempted (Heb. 4:15). Having humbled Himself to become a human being, Jesus honors the Father as His God, even after His resurrection (John 20:17; Rev. 3:12).

To summarize: Jesus is the eternal Son of God, who becomes the God-Man in the Incarnation. As divine yet completely human, He fulfills the law, honoring the Father as God. So now, it should begin to make sense that both Paul and Peter refer to Yahweh as the "God and Father of our Lord Jesus Christ."

THE FATHER OF ISRAEL

The Israelites enjoy a unique relationship with Yahweh, who creates a nation for Himself out of the pagan tribes of the world. Then, He calls Himself the Father of Israel. This special relationship is anchored in God's sovereign will and eternal plan to deliver the redemption of sinful mankind through a special people marked off as His own. While the Israelites enjoy great benefits as the "firstborn" of Yahweh (Exod. 4:22), they may claim no merit of their own in this unique relationship. In fact, they often come under the chastening hand of their Father when they violate the terms of their covenant with Yahweh.

In a terse warning to the Israelites, Moses contrasts the faithfulness of God with the once and future corruption of His people: "Is this how you repay the Lord, you foolish and senseless people? Isn't he your Father and Creator? Didn't he make you and sustain you? Remember the days of old; consider the years of past generations. Ask your father, and he will tell you, your elders, and they will teach you. When the Most High gave the nations their inheritance and divided the human race, he set the boundaries of the peoples according to the number of the people of Israel. But the Lord's portion is his people, Jacob, his own inheritance" (Deut. 32:6-9).

Isaiah may have this passage in mind as he prays, "Yet Lord, you are our Father; we are the clay, and you are our potter; we all are the work of your hands" (Isa. 64:8).

Other Old Testament passages tell us of the special relationship between Yahweh and Israel. After receiving contributions for the temple that his son, Solomon, would build, David blesses the Lord in the presence of the entire assembly: "May you be blessed, Lord God of our father Israel, from eternity to eternity. Yours, Lord, is the greatness and the power and the glory and the splendor and the majesty, for everything in the heavens and on earth belongs to you. Yours, Lord, is the kingdom, and you are exalted as head over all. Riches and honor come from you, and you are the ruler of everything. Power and might are in your hand, and it is in your hand to make great and to give strength to all. Now, therefore, our God, we give you thanks and praise your glorious name" (1 Chron. 29:10-13).

In Isaiah 63, the prophet apparently quotes a prayer of the people, who wrongly claim that the Lord has caused them to stray. Even so, they acknowledge His fatherhood: "You, Lord, are our Father; your name is Our Redeemer from Ancient Times" (Isa. 63:16). And the prophet Malachi, in a stern warning to the men of Judah about marrying foreign wives who worship pagan gods, reminds them, "Don't all of us have one Father? Didn't one God create us?" (Mal. 2:10).

Yahweh is the Father of Israel in two senses. First, He is the Father of the nation as a whole. The Lord instructs Moses to tell Pharaoh, "This is what the Lord says: Israel is my firstborn son. I told you: Let my son go so that he may worship me, but you refused to let him go" (Exod. 4:22-23). Second, Yahweh is the Father of individual sons of God. As Moses spells out forbidden practices that mimic the pagan nations around them, he assures the people, "You are the sons of the Lord your God" (Deut. 14:1).

This special relationship between Yahweh and the Israelites, of course, does not mean that every Israelite automatically inherits everlasting life. Quite the contrary. After spelling out the benefits of being Yahweh's firstborn, the apostle Paul offers some tough love to his Jewish readers: "Now it is not as though the word of God has failed, because not all who are descended from Israel are Israel. Neither are all of Abraham's children his descendants. On the contrary, your offspring will be traced through Isaac. That is, it is not the children by physical descent who are God's children, but the children of the promise are considered to be the offspring" (Rom. 9:6-8).

Paul goes on to write that Gentiles may call God their Father because they have pursued righteousness by faith rather than by the works of the law (vv. 30-33). This leads to the final reality in this chapter – God as the Father of the church.

THE FATHER OF THE CHURCH

Finally, let's consider the wonderful doctrine of God as Father of the church – specifically, as the Father of everyone who receives His Son, Jesus Christ, by faith and thus is adopted into God's family.

The Bible speaks of adoption as an act of God making born-again believers members of His family. As in first-century Roman culture, all former relationships of the adopted child are severed, and the adoptee is made a full-fledged member of his or her family under the father's authority, and with the full privileges and responsibilities of an adult. No longer does the evil one hold his servants captive, in spiritual blindness, alienated from God, and destined for outer darkness. Christ has come to our rescue, redeeming us from the slave market of sin and joyfully welcoming us into the Father's family as Jesus' coheirs in His everlasting kingdom.

Adoption into God's family is part of the Father's predestined plan for everyone who believes. It is inextricably bound to all other elements of salvation, spanning from eternity past in foreknowledge to eternity future in glorification. As a consequence, we may rest assured of our salvation, for just as a Roman father could not disown an adopted son, God is faithful to His promise to conform us to the image of His eternal Son.

Consider a few New Testament passages that describe the believer's relationship with his or her Heavenly Father:

Romans 8:14-17 – "For all those led by God's Spirit are God's sons. You did not receive a spirit of slavery to fall back into fear. Instead, you received the Spirit of adoption, by whom we cry out, '*Abba*, Father!' The Spirit himself testifies together with our spirit that we are God's children, and if children, also heirs – heirs of God and coheirs with Christ – if indeed we suffer with him so that we may also be glorified with him."

These verses show the cooperative work of the triune Godhead in adoption, with the Spirit leading, indwelling, and testifying to the finished work of Christ. As a result, born-again believers may rightly consider ourselves coheirs of all things with Jesus, and together we may call the Father *Abba* – our Papa.

Galatians 4:4-5 – "When the time came to completion, God sent his Son, born of a woman, born under the law, to redeem those under the law, so that we might receive adoption as sons."

The adoption of believing people as children of God is conditioned on the finished work of Christ. Paul reminds us that the Son's appearance on earth comes at exactly the right moment. Just as the Father appoints a day for His Son to come to earth as the Lamb of God who takes away the sin of the world (John 1:29), He also governs human history in such a way that the birth of Jesus coincides with the world's readiness for a Redeemer.[3]

Not only does the Son's appearance on earth come at exactly the right moment, it comes in a most unusual way. Jesus is "born of a woman" (Gal. 4:4), a reference to His miraculous conception in a virgin's womb. Further, Jesus is "born under the law, to redeem those under the law" (vv. 4-5). To redeem is to set free by paying a price. Our Redeemer is born under the Mosaic Law. Rather than do away with the law, He fulfills it through His sinless life, which is then offered up for us (Rom. 5:17; 2 Cor. 5:21; Heb. 4:15-16). This satisfies God's justice and extends to us His grace and mercy. What's more, we now become the adopted children of the Father.

Ephesians 1:5-6 – "He predestined us to be adopted as sons through Jesus Christ for himself, according to the good pleasure of his will, to the praise of his glorious grace that he lavished on us in the Beloved One."

While our adoption as children of God takes place in time – after we are born again – it always has been in the mind of God. Just as the Father chose us in Christ before the foundation of the world (v. 4), He also predestined us to be adopted as His sons and daughters. In the New Testament, the Greek word *proorizo* consistently refers to God's predetermined plan to bring salvation history to its climax in the person of Jesus Christ, "the Beloved One" (v. 6). God the Father always is the subject of this verb in the New Testament.[4]

Because God's plan of salvation is eternal and intersects with us in time, we may rest assured of our security in Christ. As Robert Utley writes, "A Roman father had the legal right to disinherit or even kill natural children, but not adopted children. This reflects the believer's security in Christ."[5]

This is a breathtaking truth. Just as it pleased God the Father to smite His own (eternal, un-adopted) Son on our behalf (Isa. 53:10), He adopts us "according to the good pleasure of his will" (Eph. 1:5). Not that Jesus is a victim in this divine plan, for the Son of Man makes it clear that He comes into the world to give His life as a ransom for many (Matt. 20:28). He voluntarily lays down His life (John 10:17-18). And, for joy, He endures the cross (Heb. 12:2).

There is no sibling rivalry here between the natural heir of all things and the coheirs His Father has adopted into the family. The Father and Son (and the Spirit) are on the same page. What a remarkable story of divine love and sacrifice for the sake of our adoption.

Michael Bauman offers several key insights into the Fatherhood of God: "When Jesus revealed God to us – and God is revealed nowhere so clearly and so fully as in Christ – the God revealed to us was revealed as Father, and nothing else except as Father. Christ speaks of Him in that way some 160 times. The only time Jesus spoke to Him in any other way was the cry of dereliction from the cross, itself a quotation from the Old Testament. Furthermore, when Jesus taught us to pray, He taught us to begin all our prayers by acknowledging God as our Father."

He adds: "When Christ told us that to see Him was to see the Father, we learned that fatherhood is something expressed in humility, obedience, service, purity, innocent suffering, honorable death, and victory over sin and the grave. Divine fatherhood, in other words, is love and power exercised on behalf of others. The bond between the Father and us is no longer merely what it was in the Old Testament era. The God of Israel has become our *abba*" [an ancient Aramaic word we may render "Papa"].

Last, Bauman writes: "God's fatherhood is perhaps the most fundamental thing about Him. That is why He is constantly making us – each of us – His children. That is why He is constantly desiring to make a family of us. He will not relent until He has succeeded.... As the adopted children of God, we claim membership in a family much more extensive, important, and enduring than the human family from which we sprang. To confess belief in God the Father, therefore, is to affirm belief in an ultimately benevolent universe. To confess belief in God the Father is to affirm that you are no mere cog in a mindless machine; you are a child in your Father's home."[6]

REVIEW

1. While God the Father is a person, He is not _____.
The Bible explicitly denies that the Father is a man, and it affirms His divine, eternal nature as _____.
When the Bible tells us that no one has seen God, it is a refer-

ence to the _____, who is spirit (John 1:18; 4:24). However, Jesus is "the radiance [or reflection] of God's glory and an exact _____ of his nature" (Heb. 1:3). Jesus puts it more plainly when He tells Philip, "The one who has seen me has seen the _____" (John 14:9).

2. The Bible describes the Father as God in many ways:

(a) The Greek word _____ is used of the Father.

(b) The Father's divine _____ reveal His deity.

(c) The Father performs the _____ of God.

(d) The Father _____ the words of God.

(e) The Father is _____ as God.

(f) Jesus declares the _____ of God.

(g) The Bible reveals God as the Father of all _____.

3. While Jesus assures His followers that God is their Heavenly Father, Jesus alone shares a unique _____ with the Father as the eternal Son of God. There is an intimacy in this union that only exists between two eternal, all-powerful, all-knowing _____.

4. The Israelites enjoy a unique relationship with Yahweh, who creates a _____ for Himself out of the pagan tribes of the world. Then, He calls Himself the _____

of Israel. This special relationship is anchored in God's sovereign will and eternal plan to deliver the _____ of sinful mankind through a special people marked off as His own.

5. There is a sense in which Yahweh is the Father of the church – specifically, as the Father of everyone who _____ His Son, Jesus Christ, by faith and thus is _____ into God's family. Christ has come to our rescue, redeeming us from the slave _____ of sin and joyfully welcoming us into the Father's _____ as Jesus' coheirs in His everlasting kingdom.

THINK

Questions for personal or group study

1. Many counterfeit forms of Christianity profess belief in the fatherhood of God, yet they fail to express this doctrine biblically. Consider:

- Why can't the God of Jehovah's Witnesses be an *eternal* Father?
- Why is the Heavenly Father of Latter-day Saints not the *only* Heavenly Father in existence?
- And why can't the Father that United Pentecostals worship be distinguished from the Son?

2. Read John 1:18. If no one has ever seen God, how can John say that Jesus *is* God? And where does the Father fit into this discussion? Consider this verse in the context of John 1:1-18.

3. What are some ways the Bible describes the Father as God? How do these descriptions make Him different from all other fathers? At the same time, how does the name "Father" help us better understand our relationship with God?

4. New Testament writers Paul and Peter both use the phrase "the God and Father of our Lord Jesus Christ." How is it that Yahweh is both the God of Jesus, and His Father?

5. How do the following New Testament passages describe the Christian's relationship with God the Father:

Romans 8:14-17

_____

_____

_____

Galatians 4:4-5

_____

_____

_____

Ephesians 1:5-6

_____

_____

_____

Jesus serves as the fulcrum upon which the Trinity's self-revelation rests. If Jesus is not divine, the doctrine of the Trinity is false and we are driven to the alternative explanations that Jehovah's Witnesses, Muslims, and others offer. Worse, we descend into despair, for if Jesus is not divine, He cannot be the Messiah, which means we are still dead in our sins.

CHAPTER SIX

The Son is God

It's hard to imagine a teaching about Jesus more hotly contested than His deity. But this is nothing new. Even a cursory reading of the Gospels places us squarely into a first-century fray. The way Jesus speaks about Himself and acts – claiming equality with the Father, receiving worship, and forgiving sins – convinces many of His deity, while causing others to reject Him as a false prophet, or worse, a madman. Ultimately, the religious leaders accuse Jesus of blasphemy and cry out for His crucifixion.

That doesn't end the debate. In the early decades of the church, while the New Testament is still being penned, the apostle John counters Docetics, who misrepresent Jesus' divine nature while denying His humanity. And the writer of Hebrews finds it necessary to explain that Jesus is far superior to prophets and angels. He is, in fact, "the radiance of God's glory and the exact expression of his nature" (Heb. 1:3).

It gets worse for orthodoxy. A heretic named Arius nearly wrecks the church in the fourth century with his articulate lie that Jesus is a lesser god, but not God incarnate. Muhammad bursts onto the scene in the seventh century, claiming to restore true monotheism through Islam, while persecuting "polytheists" (Christians) for worshiping the prophet Jesus, whom Muhammad claims is merely a human messenger.

Today, Jehovah's Witnesses profess Jesus as a created being, a "god," even "mighty god," but not God Himself. Others openly admire Jesus as a role model, visionary, or reformer, but they blanch at the very notion of His deity. Nevertheless, as Jesus makes clear to His disciples gathered around Him at the foot of Mt. Hermon, it isn't good enough to have a high opinion of Jesus. We must rightly answer the most important question Jesus ever asked: "Who do you say that I am?" (Matt. 16:15).

In this chapter, we explore the deity of Jesus before moving on to the Incarnation in Chapter Seven. We begin with a look into the Old Testament. While the Gospels and the epistles abound with evidence of the deity of Christ, it may surprise you to know that the Old Testament presents a robust picture of an eternal person depicted as Yahweh and yet distinct from Him – what ancient Israelites understood to be a visible manifestation of the one true God.

OLD TESTAMENT CLUES

Prophetic portions of the Old Testament anticipate a coming Messiah. While explicit references to deity are rare, key passages offer clues of the Anointed One's eternal nature and divine power. Isaiah 9:6-7 is one example: "For a child will be born for us, a son will be given to us, and the government will be on his shoulders. He will be named Wonderful Counselor, Mighty God, Eternal Father, Prince of Peace. The dominion will be vast, and its prosperity will never end. He will reign on the throne of David and over his kingdom, to establish and sustain it with justice and righteousness from now on and forever. The zeal of the Lord of Armies will accomplish this."

Since the Israelites are strict monotheists, the very idea of "Mighty God, Eternal Father" coming to sit on King David's throne and rule forever no doubt fuels great wonder and encouragement in God's people. The name "Mighty God" means more than a godlike person or hero, for the same Hebrew term, *El Gibhor*, is applied elsewhere in the Old Testament to Yahweh (for example, Isa. 10:21; Jer. 32:18). Isaiah understands that the Messiah is God in the same sense of the term.

As for "Everlasting Father," Isaiah does not mean to confuse the Father and the Messiah as if they are the same person. Rather, the prophet uses a Jewish idiom to describe the Messiah's relationship to time, not His relationship with the other members of the Trinity. The Messiah is everlasting, just as God the Father is called the "Ancient of Days" in Daniel 7:9. It is similar to Micah's Messianic prophecy, which declares, "His origin is from antiquity, from ancient times" (Mic. 5:2).

Consider some additional Old Testament passages:

Psalm 45:6-7 Your throne, God, is forever and ever; the scepter of your kingdom is a scepter of justice. You love righteousness and hate wickedness; therefore God, your God, has anointed you with the oil of joy more than your companions."

This psalm celebrates the wedding of a king from the house of David. But not just any king. This psalm anticipates the Messiah, whom the psalmist calls "God" while distinguishing Him from "your God." The writer of Hebrews applies this Psalm to Jesus, whom God the Father addresses as "God" (Heb. 1:8-9).

Psalm 102:25-27 – "Long ago you established the earth, and the heavens are the work of your hands. They will perish, but you will endure; all of them will wear out like clothing. You will change them like a garment, and they will pass away. But you are the same, and your years will never end."

Near the end of this heartbroken prayer for aid, the psalmist acknowledges the eternal nature of God. The writer of Hebrews ties Jesus to this psalm, calling Him "Lord" and confirming Him as Creator: "In the beginning, Lord, you established the earth, and the heavens are the works of your hands" (Heb. 1:10).

Daniel 7:9, 13-14 – "As I kept watching, thrones were set in place, and the Ancient of Days took his seat. His clothing was white like snow, and the hair of his head like whitest wool. His throne was flaming fire; its wheels were blazing fire" (v. 9).

Four verses later, Daniel writes, "I continued watching in the night visions, and suddenly one like a son of man was coming with the clouds of heaven. He approached the Ancient of Days and was escorted before him. He was given dominion, and glory, and a kingdom; so that those of every people, nation, and language should serve him. His dominion is an everlasting dominion that will not pass away, and his kingdom is one that will not be destroyed" (vv. 13-14).

While some interpret "one like a son of man" as an angel (Michael), and others see him as a personification of the people of God (Israel), Jesus connects Himself to this passage. In fact, He refers to Himself as the Son of Man some eighty times in the Gospels. Early postbiblical Jewish writings also reflect the Messianic view.[1]

Caiaphas, the high priest, asks Jesus, "Are you the Messiah, the Son of the Blessed One?" Jesus replies, "I am ... and you will see the Son of Man seated at the right hand of Power and coming with the clouds of heaven" (Mark 14:61-62). The high priest tears his robes and says, "Why do we still need witnesses? You have heard the blasphemy" (vv. 63-64). This affirms Caiaphas' understanding of the "son of man" in Daniel 7:13 as a divine person.

It's important to note that Jesus' self-understanding is steeped in Old Testament prophecies. For example, Jesus claims that God's angels are His angels (Matt. 13:41; Luke 12:8-9) and that God's kingdom is His kingdom (Matt. 19:23-

24; John 18:36). He also makes it clear that all judgment is His (John 5:22).

Further, He applies several Old Testament references of divinity to Himself. When the children gathered in the temple shout, "Hosanna to the Son of David," prompting the chief priests and scribes to react in rage, Jesus responds by applying Psalm 8:2 to Himself: "Yes, have you never read: You have prepared praise from the mouths of infants and nursing babies?" (Matt. 21:16).

At another time, Jesus identifies the tenant farmers in the parable of the vineyard owner with the chief priests and scribes of His day, pointing them to Psalm 118:22 and Isaiah 8:14-15: "But he looked at them and said, 'Then what is the meaning of this Scripture: The stone that the builders rejected has become the cornerstone? Everyone who falls on that stone will be broken to pieces, but on whomever it falls, it will shatter him'" (Luke 20:17-18). The application of the parable is clear: Jesus is the Son who is killed, prompting divine retribution.

Jesus applies the prophecies of Elijah, the forerunner of Yahweh, to John the Baptist, thus declaring Himself the Lord who comes in judgment (Mal. 3:1; 4:5-6; Matt. 11:10-15). And the judgment scene that Jesus describes in Matthew 25:31-46 harks back to several Old Testament passages foretelling a day of Yahweh's judgment (Dan. 7:9-10; Joel 3:1-16; Zech. 14:4ff).

No doubt, Jesus and the New Testament writers see the threads of Old Testament Messianic prophecies in a fresh light, revealing a rich tapestry of the Messiah's eternal existence, omnipotence, and sovereignty. What's more, we may discover the preincarnate Christ in a most curious Old Testament figure known as the Angel of Yahweh.

THE ANGEL OF YAHWEH

Identified as Yahweh and yet distinct from Him, the Angel of Yahweh appears numerous times in human form throughout the Old Testament. He also makes a dramatic appearance as a voice from a burning bush (Exod. 3:1-17).

This messenger is above all others. He is not created. His name appears dozens of times in the Old Testament, but never in the same sense in the New Testament (except for a reference to Exodus 3:2 in Acts 7:30). He is called "the angel of the Lord," "commander of the Lord's army," "the God of Abraham," "Judge," and "I AM WHO I AM" – a name only the one true God ever claims.

Who is this awe-inspiring messenger? Ancient Jews believed Him to be a special angel, the highest revelation of the unseen God. Similarly, Roman Catholics generally regard the Angel of the Lord as an angelic representative of God, as do some Protestants. Many evangelicals, however, consider Him either as a manifestation of Yahweh – a *theophany*, derived from the Greek words *theos* (God) and *pheino* (to appear) – or as the preincarnate Son of God, a *Christophany*, the Lord Jesus.

We should note before going further that the Hebrew word *malak* and the Greek term *angelos*, translated "angel," mean "messenger." While angels in Scripture normally are spirit beings of higher intelligence and power than humans, there are times when the term may refer to human messengers, or to the Son of God. The context helps us determine the correct application.

The Preincarnate Christ

Norman Geisler writes, "Jesus Christ appears in the Old Testament in His preincarnate state as 'the Angel [Messenger] of the Lord' … Once the Son (Christ) came in permanent incarnate form (John 1:14), never again does *the* Angel of the

Lord appear. Angels appear, but no angel that is worshiped or claims to be God ever appears again. The Father and Holy Spirit never appear as a man. Hence, Jesus Christ, as a person, eternally existed and appeared as a man before His virginal conception on earth."[2]

Put another way, the Angel of the Lord is the *Logos*, the divine Word, the image of the invisible God who later manifests Himself as God in human flesh (John 1:14).

But why does Jesus appear in angelic/human form prior to His incarnation? John Calvin writes, "For though He [Christ] was not yet clothed with flesh, He came down, so to speak, as an intermediary in order to approach believers more intimately. Therefore, this closer intercourse gave Him the name of angel."[3]

Herbert Lockyer comments, "The eternal Son ... anticipated His incarnation and appears for the purpose of sustaining the faith and hope of His people, and of keeping before their minds the great redemption which was to take place in the fullness of time."[4]

Just as the Holy Spirit is active on the earth prior to the Day of Pentecost, so Jesus works collaboratively with the Father and the Spirit to bring a divine word, direction, and deliverance prior to His conception in a virgin's womb.

Key Appearances

The Angel of the Lord appears many times throughout the Old Testament, spanning the days from Abraham to Zechariah. A sampling:

To Hagar (Gen. 16:7-13). Banished from Abraham's tent, Hagar is sad, homeless, and alone in the wilderness when the Angel of the Lord appears to her and says, "I will greatly multiply your offspring, and they will be too many to count." Hagar recognizes the uniqueness of this angel, who claims the power of creation and knows the future. She names the one who speaks to her *El-roi* (God Sees Me) and asks, "[I]n this place have I actually seen the one who sees me?"

To Abraham and Sarah (Genesis 18). The angel, identified as "the Lord," appears with two others at Abraham's tent and declares, "I will certainly come back to you in about a year's time, and your wife Sarah will have a son! ... Is anything impossible for the Lord?" (vv. 10, 14). The same angel pronounces blessings for Abraham at the offering up of Isaac (Genesis 22).

To Jacob (Gen. 28:10-22). The angel visits Jacob in a dream, descending from a heavenly ladder at Bethel, and standing beside him. The angel says, "I am the Lord, the God of your father Abraham and the God of Isaac" (v. 13). He promises to bless Jacob with land and offspring. Even more important, through Jacob and his offspring (who we later learn is the Messiah), "all the peoples on earth will be blessed" (v. 14). When Jacob awakens, he remarks, "Surely the Lord is in this place, and I did not know it" (v. 16).

Later, Jacob encounters the angel again, although the Scriptures simply refer to him as "a man." The two wrestle until daybreak. The angel dislocates Jacob's hip and gives him a new name: Israel, which in Hebrew sounds like "he struggled with God." After the angel departs, Jacob names the place Peniel, or "face of God," for Jacob declares that he has seen God face to face, and lived (Gen. 32:24-32).

To Moses (Exodus 3). Exiled from the Egyptian court, Moses keeps his father-in-law's flock in the desert near Mt. Horeb. A thorn tree bursts into flame, yet it is not consumed. The Angel of the Lord says from the bush, "I am the God of your father, the God of Abraham, the God of Isaac, and the God of Jacob" (v. 6). Moses hides his face because he is afraid to look at God. On this historic occasion, God reveals His name as "I AM WHO I AM" (v. 14), the eternal, unchanging one.

It's fascinating to read how this divine being is identified as "the Angel of the Lord," "the Lord," "God," "the God of your father," "I AM WHO I AM," and "I AM."

To Joshua (Josh. 5:13-15). After Joshua succeeds Moses as the leader of Israel, he encounters the angel near Jericho, a drawn sword in His hand. The "captain of the host of the Lord" (v. 14 KJV) requires Joshua to express the same adoration and worship commanded of Moses. Joshua bows his face to the ground in worship and removes his sandals.

To Manoah and his wife (Judges 13). Samson's parents are honored with visits from this divine messenger, called "the angel of the Lord," who foretells the birth and character of their son. Manoah's wife describes Him as "a man of God" who looks like "the awe-inspiring angel of God" (v. 6). He is referred to as "the angel of the Lord" and "the Lord." When Manoah asks the angel His name, He replies that it is "beyond understanding" (v. 18). This is fitting since a name is more than a simple identifier in Scripture; it often expresses a person's nature and character. Certainly the nature of the triune God is beyond human comprehension. Manoah offers a sacrifice to the Lord, and the angel ascends in its flame. "We're certainly going to die," Manoah tells his wife, "because we have seen God!" (v. 22).

To Isaiah and Ezekiel (Isa. 6:1-13; Ezek. 1:1-28). Christ comes to both prophets as the Revealer of God. Both Isaiah and Ezekiel are granted special manifestations of Yahweh and His glory at the time of their formal calls to the prophetic office. Isaiah sees "the Lord seated on a high and lofty throne" (Isa. 6:1). The seraphim call Him "the Lord of Armies" whose glory "fills the whole earth" (v. 3), and Isaiah confesses, "my eyes have seen the King" (v. 5). Later, the apostle John tells us that Isaiah beheld Christ and His glory (John 12:37-41).

Ezekiel sees "visions of God" (Ezek. 1:1) that begin with a whirlwind, a huge cloud with erupting fire, and four living creatures who dart back and forth like flashes of lightning, moving wherever the Spirit directs. At last, a voice is heard above the expanse. A throne appears, with "someone who looked like a human," with an amber gleam encased in fire, and brilliant light all around Him (v. 27). Ezekiel can only say, "This was the appearance of the likeness of the Lord's glory. When I saw it, I fell facedown and heard a voice speaking" (v. 28).

To Zechariah (Zechariah 1-6). In a series of visions, Zechariah describes a glorious person presiding over the affairs of the world, performing ministries no ordinary angel could match. He exhibits the attributes of omniscience, omnipresence, and omnipotence. He is called both a man and the Angel of the Lord. In the fourth vision, the high priest, Joshua, appears before the Angel of the Lord, who is depicted as the Lord Himself. Satan is there as well, poised to accuse Joshua, but the Angel of the Lord says to Satan, "The Lord rebuke you, Satan! May the Lord who has chosen Jerusalem rebuke you!" (3:1-2).

The Angel's Distinction from Yahweh

While the Angel of the Lord often is identified as the Lord Himself, He also is distinguished from Yahweh. How can this be? Fred Dickason writes that there are four considerations that help identify the Angel of Yahweh as Christ in preincarnate appearances:

1. The second person of the Trinity, the Son, is the visible God of the New Testament (John 1:14, 18; Col. 2:8-9). Accordingly, the Son is the visible manifestation of God in the Old Testament.
2. The Angel of Yahweh no longer appears after Christ's incarnation.
3. The Angel of the Lord and Jesus both are sent by

God and have similar ministries such as revealing, guiding, and judging.
4. This angel could not be the Father or the Spirit. They never take bodily form (John 1:18; 3:8).

Dickason concludes, "The Angel of Jehovah, then, according to all the evidence, seems to be the preincarnate Son. His appearances evidence His eternal existence."[5]

THE DEITY OF CHRIST IN THE NEW TESTAMENT

While the Old Testament offers us glimpses of a second Yahweh figure – a visible manifestation of the one true God – the New Testament presents a more complete picture of the second person of the Godhead. Let's begin with Jesus Himself.

Did Jesus Ever Claim to be God?

Muslims, Jehovah's Witnesses, and atheists often argue, "Jesus never claimed to be God." They assert that Christians have corrupted or misinterpreted the New Testament, or they reject the Bible outright.

But for those willing to consider the eyewitness testimony of the New Testament writers, and the convincing evidence that their words are accurately preserved, we may point our unbelieving friends to seven ways that Jesus does, in fact, claim deity.

Jesus uses the divine expression "I am." In John 8:58, Jesus tells the religious leaders, "Truly I tell you, before Abraham was, I am." These words echo Exodus 3, where God reveals Himself to Moses in the burning bush as "I AM WHO I AM," or "YHWH" (Yahweh or Jehovah). The Jewish leaders clearly understand Jesus' declaration of deity, for immediately they pick up stones to throw at Him. Jesus uses the phrase "I am" (Greek: *ego eimi*) in several other places, either explicitly or metaphorically (John 6:20, 35, 48, 51; 8:12, 24, 28; 9:5; 10:7, 9, 11, 14; 11:25; 14:6; 15:1; 18:5).

Jesus claims equality with God. In John 10:30, Jesus states, "I and the Father are one." His frequent reference to God as Father – especially by the intimate Aramaic term *Abba*, or Papa – rankles the religious leaders. John writes, "This is why the Jews began trying all the more to kill him ... he was even calling God his own Father, making himself equal to God" (John 5:18).

In His high priestly prayer, Jesus anticipates once again sharing the glory He had with the Father before the world existed (John 17:5). This is a telling claim, for the Old Testament makes it clear that God does not share His glory with anyone else (Isa. 42:8; 48:11).

Also note that Jesus calls Himself the Son of Man some eighty times in the Gospels – a term that illuminates the Messiah's deity (see Dan. 7:13-14).

Jesus receives worship. After Jesus' resurrection, Thomas examines Jesus' hands and side and declares, "My Lord and my God" (John 20:28). Jesus commits blasphemy if He receives Thomas' worship unless He really is God. Similarly, when Jesus meets the eleven disciples in Galilee following His resurrection, Matthew records, "When they saw him, they worshiped, but some doubted" (Matt. 28:17).

Jesus forgives sins. When Jesus tells a paralytic man, "Son, your sins are forgiven," the scribes immediately think, "Why does he speak like this? He's blaspheming! Who can forgive sins but God alone?" Jesus exposes their private thoughts and demonstrates His authority to forgive sins by healing the paralyzed man. The visible miracle of healing is used to show Christ's power to perform the unseen miracle of forgiveness (Mark 2:1-12).

Jesus teaches with divine authority. In John 8, the Pharisees say to Jesus, "You are testifying about yourself. Your testimony is not valid." Jesus responds, "My judgment is true, because it is not I alone who judge, but I and the Father who sent me. Even in your law it is written that the testimony of two witnesses is true. I am the one who testifies about myself, and the Father who sent me testifies about me" (John 8:13-20).

When Jesus teaches in the synagogue at Capernaum, His listeners are astonished because He teaches as one who has *authority*, unlike the scribes (Mark 1:21-22). The Greek word *exousia*, translated "authority" in this verse, typically is used in the Bible for God's own authority. Jesus does not rely on the expertise of others. He speaks the very words of our Creator (see John 12:49-50).[6]

Jesus affirms the apostles' statements of His deity. Jesus promises the apostles that the Holy Spirit will guide them into all truth and bring to their minds the things He says and does. In effect, He confirms in advance what they write later. For example, John calls Jesus God and says He is the Creator who took on human flesh (John 1:1-3, 14). Paul tells us that in Jesus the fullness of deity dwells bodily (Col. 2:9); that He added to His deity sinless humanity (Phil. 2:5-11); and that He is the Creator (Col. 1:15-16). The writer of Hebrews declares the deity of Jesus as well (Heb. 1:1-4).

Jesus fulfills the attributes unique to God. In John 16:30, Jesus' disciples exclaim, "Now we know that you know everything" (omniscience). In Matthew 28:20, Jesus assures His followers He is with them always (omnipresence). And in Matthew 28:18, He claims all authority (omnipotence). In addition, Jesus is eternal (John 1:1), immutable (Heb. 13:8), and the judge of all people (John 5:22). Even the Father calls Jesus God (Heb. 1:8).

Finally, the names used to portray God in the Old Testament – Alpha and Omega, Lord, Savior, King, Judge, Light, Rock, Redeemer, Shepherd, Creator – are applied to Jesus in the New Testament.

The Eyewitness Testimony

So far, we've seen that Jesus claims to be God, and He proves His deity through divine acts that only Yahweh can perform. But is there corroborating testimony? What do those who know Jesus best – the disciples who walk the dusty first-century Galilean roads with Him – have to say about the issue? In reality, the pages of the New Testament ooze with the deity of Christ – and most of the writers are strict monotheistic Jews! Many respected scholars have produced excellent works that lay out for us how the first-hand testimonies unite in their proclamation of Jesus as divine.[7] In the limited scope of this study, let's consider a sampling of testimony from the apostles and other first-century eyewitnesses.

The Witness of John

No other eyewitness goes to the lengths of the apostle John to bear testimony to the deity of Jesus. Here are a few examples:

John 1:1-5 – "In the beginning was the Word, and the Word was with God, and the Word was God. He was with God in the beginning. All things were created through him, and apart from him not one thing was created that has been created. In him was life, and that life was the light of men. That light shines in the darkness, and yet the darkness did not overcome it."

In these five verses, John declares several key truths about Jesus: (1) He is eternal, existing with God "in the beginning" (cf. Gen. 1:1); (2) He is the Word – the *Logos*, the expression of divine power and wisdom; (3) He is a distinct person from God the Father; (4) He is God; (5) He is the Creator, the one who made "all things;" (6) He is life – from the Greek *zoe*, which refers to spiritual life as opposed to the Greek *bios*, which describes physical life; and (7) His life is the light of all people – God's life manifested in Christ.

John further notes, "The Word became flesh and dwelt among us. We observed his glory, the glory as the one and only Son from the Father, full of grace and truth" (John 1:14). God becomes man in the Incarnation, the topic of our next chapter, and John is among the eyewitnesses who see His unveiled glory (Matt. 17:1-8). He even declares, "No one has ever seen God. The one and only Son, who is himself God and is at the Father's side – he has revealed him" (John 1:18).

John 5:17-24 – John records Jesus' claim of deity to the religious leaders. Jesus says He does what the Father does, gives life just as the Father does, judges all things, and deserves the same honor due to the Father. John writes, "This is why the Jews began trying all the more to kill him: Not only was he breaking the Sabbath, but he was even calling God his own Father, making himself equal to God" (v. 18).

John 10:22-40 – John reports Jesus' encounter with the Jews gathered at the Festival of Dedication. Jesus calls God His Father, and claims to do works in His Father's name. He acknowledges that He is the promised Messiah. He grants eternal life. He states plainly that He and the Father are one in nature, glory, and authority. He says the Father is in Him and He is in the Father. He remarks, "I am the Son of God" (v. 36). When the Jews pick up rocks to stone Him, they say, "We aren't stoning you for a good work … but for blasphemy, because you – being a man – make yourself God" (v. 33)

1 John 5:20-21 – "And we know that the Son of God has come and has given us understanding so that we may know the true one. We are in the true one – that is, in his Son Jesus Christ. He is the true God and eternal life."

John uses the word "true" (Greek *alethinos*) three times to emphasize the value of truth in a world filled with the lies of the evil one. The last use of the word underscores the most important truth of all: Jesus is "the true God and eternal life."

Revelation 1:17-18 – "When I saw him, I fell at his feet like a dead man. He laid his right hand on me and said, 'Don't be afraid. I am the First and the Last, and the Living One. I was dead, but look – I am alive forever and ever, and I hold the keys of death and Hades.'"

After quaking in terror before the glorified Christ, John listens to Jesus as He identifies Himself. First, Jesus says "I am" – *ego eimi* in Greek, the covenant name of God (cf. Exod. 3:14). Next, Jesus tells John He is "the First and the Last," a title used of God in the Old Testament (Isa. 44:6; 48:12). Jesus repeats this title in Revelation 2:8 and 22:13. Finally, Jesus claims to be "the Living One," a term used for God throughout Scripture (e.g., Josh. 3:10; 1 Sam. 17:26; Ps. 84:2; Matt. 26:63; 2 Cor. 3:3; 1 Tim. 3:15).

Jesus' words, "I was dead, but look – I am alive forever and ever," testify to His sinless humanity as the God-Man, who died on the cross and rose physically from the dead for our salvation. As John MacArthur notes, "The living One, the eternal, self-existent God who could never die, became man and died. As Peter explains in 1 Peter 3:18, Christ was 'put to death in the flesh, but made alive in the spirit.' In His humanness He died without ceasing to live as God."[8]

The Witness of Paul

Although Paul likely had no personal encounters with Jesus prior to the crucifixion, he meets Jesus in dramatic fashion on the road to Damascus after Christ's resurrection (Acts 9:1-9). Paul's conversion, testimony, and epistles bear evidence of his conviction that Jesus was, and is, divine:

Romans 9:5 – "The ancestors are theirs [the Israelites], and from them, by physical descent, came the Christ, who is God over all, praised forever. Amen."

This text is significant for at least two reasons. First, it is the earliest New Testament writing that calls Jesus "God" (dating to about AD 57), less than thirty years after Jesus' death and resurrection.[9]

Second, the word "praised" (*eulogetos*) follows the word for God (*theos*) in the Greek text. This is unusual, for without exception in Scripture, a doxology places the word "praised" (or "blessed") *before* the name of God. Here, Paul uses the reverse form, indicating that he intentionally equates Christ with God.[10]

Philippians 2:5-6 – "Adopt the same attitude as that of Christ Jesus, who, existing in the form of God, did not consider equality with God as something to be exploited."

In the Incarnation, the eternal Son of God sets aside, not His deity, but His privileged position in heaven at the Father's right hand, humbling Himself as He takes on human flesh. Before, during, and after coming to earth, Jesus is, by His very nature, fully and eternally God. Paul's use of the word "existing" (Greek *huparcho*) describes the continuation of a previous state or existence. William Barclay notes that the verb refers to "that part of a [person] which, in any circumstances, remains the same."[11]

In describing Jesus as being in the "form" of God, Paul uses the Greek *morphe* rather than *schema*. This is significant. *Schema* is an outward shape that is subject to change, while *morphe* is the essential form that doesn't change. In other words, Paul tells us that Jesus' deity is eternal and unchanging. Barclay provides this example: "A baby, a child, a boy, a youth, a man of middle age, an old man always have the *morphe* of humanity, but the outward *schema* changes all the time."[12]

While we explore the divine and human natures of Jesus in Chapter Seven, it's important to note that throughout His time on earth, Jesus never denies His deity. He consistently maintains His equality with the Father. Yet, as Paul notes, Jesus never uses His divine authority for personal gain; that is, He does not "consider equality with God as something to be exploited" (Phil. 2:6).

Robert Bowman and Ed Komoszewski write, "Paul is saying that Christ was divine in his nature or glorious form but did not act in the self-serving manner one might have expected an omnipotent deity to act, taking whatever he wanted and demanding to be treated as a superior.... Paul's point is that although Christ was in God's form and was (at least by right) God's equal, he did not demand his divine rights but humbly took a servant's form and became a human being.... We have here, then, dating from less than twenty-five years after Jesus' death and resurrection, an apostolic writing affirming the belief in Christ's divine preexistence."[13]

Colossians 1:15-17 – "He is the image of the invisible God, the firstborn over all creation. For everything was created by him, in heaven and on earth, the visible and the invisible, whether thrones or dominions or rulers or authorities — all things have been created through him and for him. He is before all things, and by him all things hold together."

Heretical doctrines in Colossae centered around the person of Jesus Christ. They denied His full deity, depicting Him as one of the many lesser spirit beings emanating from God. Their false views of Jesus led to a skewed understanding of salvation – a salvation that required the acquisition of secret knowledge, the worship of angels, and a strict adherence to Jewish ceremonial laws.

Paul confronts all of this in his epistle, but he focuses most sharply on defending the deity of Christ. First, the apostle refers to Jesus as "the image of the invisible God." The Greek word rendered "image" is *eikon*, from which we get "icon." It means likeness. It is used in Matthew 22:20 of Caesar's face on a coin, and in Revelation 13:14 of the statue of the Antichrist. In other words, Jesus is the visible, physical manifestation of the invisible God. He is the final and complete revelation of God, the "entire fullness of God's nature" dwelling in a physical body (Col. 2:9).

Further, Paul emphasizes that "everything ... all things

have been created through him and for him." This is an echo of John 1:3, which states, "All things were created through him, and apart from him not one thing was created that has been created." Paul leaves no room for doubt about Jesus' role as Creator and the omnipotent sustainer of all things. We address Jesus as the "firstborn over all creation" later in this chapter.

Colossians 2:9-10 – "For the entire fullness of God's nature dwells bodily in Christ, and you have been filled by him, who is the head over every ruler and authority."

Paul uses a precise term in defending the deity of Christ to the heretics of Colossae. The word "fullness" in the Greek is *pleroma*. Those denying Christ's deity and humanity used this term to describe how the divine *pleroma*, or fullness of God, is divided among his various emanations, or lesser spirit beings. But Paul counters this errant doctrine by stating plainly that Jesus is fully divine – God in human skin.

Paul further uses the word "dwells" (Greek: *katoikeo*), which means "to settle down and be at home." The present tense of the verb illustrates that Christ's deity continuously resides in His human body.

Titus 2:13 – "... while we wait for the blessed hope, the appearing of the glory of our great God and Savior, Jesus Christ."

This is one of the strongest declarations of the deity of Christ in Scripture. A few English translations blur the clarity of this passage, either unintentionally or intentionally, leaving the reader to wonder whether "God" and "Savior" are two separate beings. The KJV, for example, translates the verse, "Looking for that blessed hope, and the glorious appearing of the great God and our Saviour Jesus Christ."

Not surprisingly, the New World Translation (NWT) of the Jehovah's Witnesses renders it, "[W]hile we wait for the happy hope and glorious manifestation of the great God and of our Savior, Jesus Christ."

However, it's clear that Paul is referring to Jesus as both God and Savior, for several reasons. First, there is one definite article ("the," *tou*) applied to "God" and "Savior," indicating a reference to a single person.[14] Next, the verse following uses singular pronouns as it refers back to "God" and "Savior." Verse 14 reads, "He gave himself for us to redeem us from all lawlessness and to cleanse for himself a people for his own possession, eager to do good works."

Third, although the Old Testament often refers to God the Father as "great," the New Testament writers use "great" only in regard to Jesus the Son (e.g., Matt. 5:35; Luke 1:32; Heb. 10:21). Finally, nowhere does the New Testament foretell the return of the Father. Rather, it's the second coming of Jesus to which we look forward.

The Witness of the Author of Hebrews

Hebrews 1:2-3 – "In these last days, he has spoken to us by his Son. God has appointed him heir of all things and made the universe through him. The Son is the radiance of God's glory and the exact expression of his nature, sustaining all things by his powerful word. After making purification for sins, he sat down at the right hand of the Majesty on high."

Note several truths about Christ's deity in these verses. First, God made the universe through Jesus. That is, Jesus is the Creator. When the writer of Hebrews says "through him," he does not mean that Jesus is a secondary cause of creation; rather, Jesus is the agent through whom the triune God made everything (see Chapter Nine: The Trinity in Creation). This verse corresponds with the testimony of John, who writes, "All things were created through him, and apart from him not one thing was created that has been created" (John 1:3).

Next, the writer tells us that the universe (*aionas*) was made through Jesus. This word means more than *kosmos*, or the material world. It may be rendered "ages," and it means that

Jesus is responsible for the existence of time, space, energy, matter – and even the unseen spiritual realm.

Then, in verse 3, we are told that Jesus is the "radiance of God's glory." That is, Jesus is the visible manifestation of the invisible God. The author uses the Greek word *apaugasma*, a sending forth of the light. Just as no one may gaze for long into the noonday sun without suffering visual impairment, or even blindness, no mortal human being may see the unveiled glory of God and live. Yet, like the light and warmth of the sun's rays, Jesus is deity clothed in human skin. He is "the light of the world. Anyone who follows me will never walk in the darkness but will have the light of life" (John 8:12).

The author of Hebrews goes on to describe Jesus as "the exact expression" of God's nature. The Greek word rendered "expression" is *charakter*, used to describe the impression made by a stamp or a die on steel. Put another way, Jesus is the precise imprint of deity in human form, the perfect, personal emblem of divinity. This reminds us of Paul's words in Colossians 1:15: "He is the image (*eikon*) of the invisible God."

Finally, the writer assures us that Jesus is "sustaining all things by his powerful word." This is in the present tense. The same Creator who called everything into existence now holds everything together in divine sovereignty. The appointed Heir of all things keeps all things in place through His omnipotence, omniscience, and omnipresence.

Hebrews 1:8-9 – "… but to the Son: Your throne, O God, is forever and ever, and the scepter of your kingdom is a scepter of justice. You have loved righteousness and hated lawlessness; this is why God, your God, has anointed you with the oil of joy beyond your companions."

This is perhaps the most stunning statement of Christ's deity in all of Scripture because it comes from the lips of God the Father. It is a quotation from Psalm 45:6-7, and it affirms the many statements Jesus made concerning His deity throughout the Gospels. Like His throne, Jesus' existence is eternal, and He rules His kingdom in justice.

Some may object that Psalm 45, in its original context, addresses the king of Israel, perhaps Solomon. Robert Bowman and Ed Komoszewski respond: "The Israelite king was not, of course, literally God. Like Isaiah's prophecy about a boy named Immanuel who prefigured the Messiah, who really would be 'God with us' (Isa. 7:14; Matt. 1:22-23), the psalm speaks in the immediate 'horizon' about the Jerusalem king who also prefigured the Messiah, the ultimate descendant of David and the true eternal King. We should note that the psalm does not identify the specific king, and the whole psalm may be interpreted messianically.... Psalm 45 points forward to a coming king who really would be God."[15]

Even so, if the writer means to call Jesus "God," why is God called "your God"? As in John's writings, affirmations of Jesus as God, and of the Father as Jesus' God, are placed side by side with no sense of contradiction (e.g., John 20:17, 28; Heb. 1:8, 9). Through the Incarnation, Jesus became a human being, part of the created order, and as such He properly honors the Father as God (see Rev. 3:12).

The Witness of Peter

2 Peter 1:1 – "Simeon Peter, a servant and an apostle of Jesus Christ: To those who have received a faith equal to ours through the righteousness of our God and Savior Jesus Christ."

As with Paul in Titus 2:13, Peter places a single article ("the," *tou*) before the phrase "God and Savior," establishing that both nouns apply to the same person. In this passage, however, Peter focuses, not on the return of Christ, but on His righteousness. Through the finished work of Jesus on the cross, God the Father "made the one who did not know sin to be sin for us, so that in him we might become the righteousness of God" (2 Cor. 5:21).

When believing sinners trust in Jesus, our sins are *imputed*, or charged, to the account of Christ and reckoned as paid in full. At the same time, Christ's perfect righteousness is *imputed*, or transferred, to us. It is the greatest exchange of all time: our sins for His righteousness. As a result, we are justified, or declared in right standing with God.

As the prophet Isaiah puts it, "I rejoice greatly in the Lord, I exult in my God; for he has clothed me with the garments of salvation and wrapped me in a robe of righteousness, as a groom wears a turban and as a bride adorns herself with her jewels" (Isa. 61:10).

JESUS AS THE FIRSTBORN

As we have seen in this chapter, the Bible declares Jesus the eternal Son of God. Even so, why does the apostle Paul depict Him as the "firstborn over all creation" (Col. 1:15)?

Jehovah's Witnesses have a disturbing take on this. Consider how the Watch Tower renders Colossians 1:15-17 in its New World Translation: "He is the image of the invisible God, *the firstborn of all creation*; because by means of him all *other* things were created in the heavens and on earth, the things visible and the things invisible, whether they are thrones or lordships or governments or authorities. All *other* things have been created through him and for him. Also, he is before all *other* things, and by means of him all *other* things were made to exist ..." (emphasis added). Note the unjustified insertion of the word "other" before "things" four times in the NWT.

The Watch Tower's official website explains: "Jesus is very precious to Jehovah. Why? Because God created him before everything and everyone else. So Jesus is called 'the firstborn of all creation.' Jesus is also precious to Jehovah because he is the only one Jehovah created directly. That is why he is called the 'only-begotten Son.' Jesus is also the only one Jehovah used to create all other things."[16]

To summarize, Jehovah's Witnesses believe Jesus is the first created being, known as Michael the archangel, who is sent to earth temporarily as a man, then recreated as an exalted angel after his death on a torture stake and subsequent annihilation as a human being. But is this the proper way to understand Paul's meaning of *firstborn*?

In a word, no.

Firstborn in Context

There are two primary reasons the Watch Tower's interpretation of "firstborn" is deceptive. First, context. The word "firstborn" is used in a variety of ways in Scripture.

Usually, "firstborn" means the first male child born into a family, but the word can be used in other ways. It may denote rank, position, or prominence. King David, for example, who is the last in his family's birth order, is called "firstborn, greatest of the kings of the earth" (Ps. 89:27).

The same is true for the nation of Israel. The Israelites are not the first people group to populate a region of the earth. Even so, the Lord tells Moses to tell pharaoh that "Israel is my firstborn son" (Exod. 4:22). That is, God established the Israelites as a special people for whom the Promised Land is prepared.

These examples show that birth order is not always in view when writers of Scripture use the word "firstborn." What's more, the context of Colossians 1:15-17 makes it clear that Jesus is the Creator who is "before all things."

The New World Translation's use of the word "other" numerous times in these verses is unwarranted. Earlier versions of the NWT bracketed the word "other" and argued that "other" is implied, but the 2013 revision boldly leaves the brackets off. "This amounts to nothing less than academic dishonesty, because the word *other* neither exists in the original nor is implied by anything else in the text," writes Eric Bargerhuff.[17]

Paul clearly describes Jesus as the Creator who is "before all things" and by whom "all things hold together."

Doctrine Before Scripture

A second reason Jehovah's Witnesses are guilty of deception is because they have imposed their errant doctrine on Scripture rather than allowing God's Word to speak for itself. If Paul had meant to say that Jesus was a created being in Colossians 1:15, he could have used the Greek word *protoktisis* rather than *prototokos*.

Renowned Bible scholar F. F. Bruce writes, "The word first-born had long since ceased to be used exclusively in its literal sense, just as *prime* (from the Latin word *primus* - 'first') with us. The Prime Minister is not the first minister we have had; he is the most preeminent.... Similarly, first-born came to denote [among the ancients] not priority in time but preeminence in rank."[18]

As firstborn, the fullness of deity always has rested in Christ (Col. 1:19; 2:9). There has never been a time when Jesus did not exist or was not God.

Once you deny a clear doctrine of Scripture, you may find it necessary to alter Scripture to conform it to your beliefs. That's why Jehovah's Witnesses use the NWT to equate Jesus with created wisdom (Proverbs 8); reduce Him to "a god" (John 1:1 NWT); deny He is the "I AM" by calling Him the "I have been" (John 8:58 NWT); and say "God is your throne" (Heb. 1:8 NWT) rather than "Your throne, O God, is forever and ever" (CSB).

These are dangerous deceptions that deny the deity of the "firstborn over all creation."

JESUS AS THE ONLY BEGOTTEN

Another way Jehovah's Witnesses seek to deny the deity of Christ is through their misuse of the term "only begotten," which appears several times in the Gospel of John, most notably in John 3:16: "For God so loved the world, that he gave his only begotten Son, that whosoever believeth in him should not perish, but have everlasting life" (KJV). Many modern translations render the term "one and only Son," emphasizing Christ's uniqueness.

Jehovah's Witnesses argue that "only begotten" means Jesus is the only direct creation of Jehovah, who then created all other things through His Son. The key is the Greek word *monogenes*. James White explains how linguistic studies and the discovery of ancient papyri in the Egyptian deserts within the last century have clarified a proper understanding of this term:

> It was assumed that the term was made up of two parts: *monos*, which means "only," and *gennao*, which is a verb meaning "to beget, give birth to." The assumption was half correct. *Monogenes* does come from *monos* but not from *gennao*; rather, the second part of the word comes from a noun, *genos*, that means "kind" or "type." Therefore, *monogenes* means "one of a kind, unique" rather than "only begotten," and, accordingly, the term was used of an only son, a unique son. The importance for Christology is clear: No one can base a denial of the Son's eternal nature upon this term, for it does not refer to a "beginning" at all but instead describes the uniqueness of the object.[19]

The apostle John, who takes great care to establish the deity of Jesus, wants us to know that while Jesus is the Son of God, His Sonship is an eternal, one-of-a-kind relationship with God the Father. Believing sinners are "begotten" in the sense that we are born again, or made spiritually alive through the regenerating work of the Holy Spirit. Our sonship is through adoption; Christ's Sonship is by the very nature of His eternal relationship with the Father.

WAS JESUS ALWAYS THE SON OF GOD?

A final thought is in order here. When the Bible says that Jesus is the Son of God, does it mean Jesus *always* was the Son, or that He *became* the Son at some point in time, such as His incarnation or baptism? This brings us to the doctrine of the eternal Sonship of Jesus.

The doctrine of eternal Sonship affirms that the second person of the Trinity exists eternally as the Son. Put another way, there has always been a Father / Son relationship within the Godhead, and there never was a time when Jesus was not the Son of God. The idea of Sonship is not a title or a role that Jesus assumed at some point in history; that is what's known as "incarnational Sonship." Rather, it is the essential identity of the second person of the triune Godhead.

We normally think of father-son relationships requiring procreation, with the father existing before his child. Yet, the word "son" as it's used of Jesus in Scripture aims more at describing similarities between two eternal persons. Just as a human father enjoys a relationship with a human son, so God the Father enjoys an eternal relationship with His divine Son.

It might also help to consider that Jesus could not become the Son of God at some point in history, because that would mean God could not be an eternal Father, even though the Bible depicts Him as such. His fatherhood, in other words, would be contingent on the Son, and Jesus' Sonship would be contingent on the Father. But God's unchanging nature does not hinge on anything.

Consider a few ways in which the Bible bears evidence of Christ's eternal Sonship:

The Son is the Creator. Paul writes that the *Son* created everything in heaven and on earth, and that He is before all things (Col. 1:13-17). The writer of Hebrews tells us that God made the universe through His *Son* (Heb. 1:2). These passages strongly imply that Christ is the Son at the time of creation.

The Father sends the Son into the world. Numerous New Testament verses speak of God the Father sending His Son to redeem sinful people. For example, John writes, "God's love was revealed among us in this way: God sent his one and only Son into the world so that we might live through him. Love consists in this: not that we loved God, but that he loved us and sent his Son to be the atoning sacrifice for our sins.... And we have seen and we testify that the Father has sent his Son as the world's Savior" (1 John 4:9-10, 14).

Clearly, Jesus is the Son before He is sent into the world. This is made even more clear in Galatians 4:4-6, where the verb "sent" is used both of the Son and the Holy Spirit. All three persons of the Trinity have existed for all eternity. Their names reveal who they are, not merely their titles or functions.

The Son is revealed. John writes, "The Son of God was revealed for this purpose: to destroy the devil's works" (1 John 3:8). The verb "revealed" means to make visible or bring to light something previously hidden. This shows us the Son did not come into being, but that He became incarnate in order to fulfill the Father's purpose. (See also John 11:27 and 1 John 5:20.)

The Son comes from the Father. Jesus tells His disciples, "I came from the Father and have come into the world. Again, I am leaving the world and going to the Father" (John 16:28). This implies that the Father / Son relationship existed long before the Incarnation and would continue long after it. Further support comes from Jesus' prayer in John 17:5: "Now, Father, glorify me in your presence with that glory I had with you before the world existed." And, "Father, I want those you have given me to be with me where I am, so that they will see my glory, which you have given me because you loved me before the world's foundation" (John 17:24).

The Scriptures reveal eternal relationships between the Father, Son, and Holy Spirit. The idea of "incarnational Sonship" – or that Jesus became the Son at some point in history – falls short of a biblically faithful understanding of the person and work of Christ. As one author explains, "Taken to its logical conclusion, denying the eternal Sonship of Christ reduces the Trinity from the relationship of Father, Son, and Holy Spirit to simply Number One, Number Two and Number Three Persons – with the numbers themselves being an arbitrary designation, destroying the God-given order and relationship that exists among the Persons of the Trinity."[20]

SUMMARY

Jesus serves as the fulcrum upon which the Trinity's self-revelation rests. If Jesus is not divine, the doctrine of the Trinity is false and we are driven to the alternative explanations that Jehovah's Witnesses, Muslims, and others offer. Worse, we descend into despair, for if Jesus is not divine, He cannot be the Messiah, which means we are still dead in our sins. But the Bible reveals both a divine Jesus and a triune Godhead.

From the earliest pages of the Old Testament, we see a divine person who bears all the marks of Yahweh yet is distinct from the invisible God. Put another way, we experience, at times, a visible manifestation of the invisible Yahweh. He comes to reveal the unique name of Yahweh; to direct human history; to bring messages; and to temporarily become like one of us – appearing in human form – that we might better relate to Him.

Even better, in the village of Bethlehem some two thousand years ago, the eternal Son of God comes permanently to us in human skin through the miracle of the virgin birth.

Without shedding His deity, or compromising the attributes of Yahweh, Jesus of Nazareth, as the God-Man, comes to save us from sin and its devastating consequences. It is to this work, the Incarnation, that we turn next.

REVIEW

1. While explicit Old Testament references to the Messiah's deity are rare, key passages like Isaiah 9:6-7 offer clues to the Anointed One's eternal _____ and divine _____: "For a child will be born for us, a son will be given to us, and the government will be on his shoulders. He will be named Wonderful Counselor, Mighty _____, Eternal _____, Prince of Peace…"

2. Identified as Yahweh and yet distinct from Him, the _____ of Yahweh appears numerous times in human form throughout the Old Testament. This messenger is above all others. He is called by many names, including "the angel of the Lord," "_____ of the Lord's army," and "I _____ WHO I AM." Evangelicals regard this messenger either as a _____ (manifestation of God), or as a _____ (an appearance of the preincarnate Lord Jesus).

3. Jesus claims deity in at least seven ways in the New Testament. Specifically, He:

(a) Uses the divine expression "I _____"

(b) Claims _____ with God

(c) Receives _____

(d) _____ sins

(e) Teaches with divine _____

(f) Affirms the _____ statements of His deity

(g) Fulfills the _____ unique to God

4. The apostles and other eyewitnesses of Jesus' earthly ministry provide strong corroborating _____ of the deity of Christ. Among these eyewitnesses are John, Paul, the writer of _____, and Peter.

5. In calling Jesus the "firstborn over all creation" (Col. 1:15), Paul does not mean that Jesus is the _____ of God's created beings. Rather, Paul's use of the Greek *prototokos* conveys the idea that the eternal Son of God is _____ over all He has made. Equally important, when John calls Jesus the "only begotten Son," he is not referring to Jesus as a direct creation of God. Instead, the Greek term *monogenes* means "one of a _____."

THINK

Questions for personal or group study

1. You're visiting with a Jehovah's Witness, who reads Colossians 1:15-17 from the New World Translation, which regards Jesus as "the firstborn of all creation" who then creates all "other" things. Your JW friend explains that this passage clearly reveals Jesus as a created being through whom Jehovah made everything else. How would you respond?

2. In what ways does the Old Testament offer clues of the coming Messiah's eternal nature and divine power? Specifically, consider:

- Psalm 45:6-7 (cf. Heb. 1:8-9)
- Psalm 102:25-27 (cf. Heb. 1:10)
- Isaiah 9:6-7
- Daniel 7:9, 13-14 (cf. Mark 14:61-64)
- The Angel of Yahweh (e.g., Gen. 22:11-18)

3. Jesus' self-understanding is steeped in Old Testament prophecies. Try to identify a few Old Testament passages that Jesus applies to Himself. For example, begin with Matthew 21:16 and Luke 20:17-18.

4. No other eyewitness goes to the lengths of the apostle John to bear testimony to the deity of Jesus. In what specific ways do the following Scriptures offer evidence of Jesus' divine nature?

John 1:1-5

John 5:17-24

John 10:22-40

1 John 5:20-21

Revelation 1:17-18

5. When the Bible says that Jesus is the Son of God, does that mean Jesus *always* was the Son, or that He *became* the Son at some point in time, such as His incarnation or baptism? What Scriptures support your point of view?

"He who sat upon the well of Sychar, and said, 'Give Me to drink,' was none other than He who dug the channels of the ocean, and poured into them the floods. Son of Mary, You are also Son of Jehovah!"

— C. H. Spurgeon

CHAPTER SEVEN

Jesus as the God-Man

Christians often find it necessary to defend the deity of Christ, especially in conversations with those who vigorously deny this biblical truth. For example, Muslims hold Jesus in high regard as a virgin-born, miracle-working, sinless prophet, but they draw the line at His divinity. Jehovah's Witnesses grant Jesus the status of "mighty god," a created archangel who later is recreated as Jesus the man, and then, after dying on a first-century torture stake, is recreated once again as an exalted archangel. Both Muslims and Jehovah's Witnesses admire Jesus. Unfortunately, they proclaim "another Jesus" than the one revealed in Scripture (2 Cor. 11:4).

Our efforts to defend the deity of Jesus, however, require us to grapple with the unique challenges His humanity presents. The Bible is clear that Jesus is the God-Man. That is, two thousand years ago, the eternal Son of God added sinless humanity to His deity through the virgin birth and thus became the only person in history with two natures: divine and human.

Critics of the orthodox view often respond with questions such as: If Jesus is God, why doesn't He know the day or hour of His return (Mark 13:32)? Why does Jesus get tired, thirsty, and hungry (Mark 11:12; John 4:6; 19:28)? Why does He insist that the Father is greater than He is (John 14:28)? And, if Jesus truly is divine, how is it possible for God to die (John 19:30)?

DIVINITY IN HUMAN SKIN

These are challenging questions. If the Incarnation means that Jesus is completely divine and completely human at the same time, never surrendering one nature to the other, how might we explain the apparent absence of divine attributes at certain times in our Savior's life?

Theologian Bruce Ware provides marvelous insight into the two natures of Christ in *The Man Christ Jesus*. He begins with an exposition of Philippians 2:5-8, which expresses the self-emptying of the eternal Son as He takes on human nature.

First, Ware notes that Paul expresses no doubts about the deity of Christ. The phrase "though he was in the form of God" (Phil. 2:6 ESV) employs the Greek word *morphe*, which refers to the inner nature or substance of something, not its external or outward shape. Therefore, Paul's point is clear: Jesus, being in the "form" of God, exists in very nature as God, with the inner divine substance that is God's alone.

Second, when Paul writes that Christ "did not count equality with God a thing to be grasped" (Phil. 2:6 ESV), he cannot mean that Christ gave up equality with God or that He ceased to be fully God. Rather, Jesus did not cling to His privileged position at the Father's right hand, or to the rights and prerogatives that go along with full equality with the Father. Instead, He fulfilled His mission as the Servant of all.

Third, Jesus "emptied himself, by taking the form of a servant" (Phil. 2:7 ESV). The Greek *ekenosen* means Christ "poured out himself." In other words, all of Christ, as eternal

God, is poured out. As Jesus becomes human, He loses nothing of His divine nature.

Fourth, Jesus "humbled himself by becoming obedient to the point of death, even death on a cross" (Phil. 2:8 ESV). Ware notes that "this is the obedience that accepts suffering, rejection, ridicule, and agony. Surely the Son, in eternity past, never had to embrace this kind of obedience in his relation to the Father…. To obey to the point of death requires the ability to die, and for this, Jesus had to be human."[1]

So, when we come to passages that tell us Jesus doesn't know something, or gets hungry or thirsty, or dies, we may understand that Jesus neither surrenders His deity nor abandons His claims of divinity. Rather, "He had to be like His brothers in every way, so that He could become a merciful and faithful high priest in service to God, to make propitiation for the sins of the people" (Heb. 2:17 HCSB).

THE DOCTRINE OF THE INCARNATION

Lorenzo Snow, fifth president of the Church of Jesus Christ of Latter-day Saints, once claimed the Spirit of God fell upon him and revealed a principle that has become an apt summary of Mormonism: "As man now is, God once was; As God now is, man may be."[2]

In other words, the LDS god of this world once was a mere human who attained deity, showing us the path to our own godhood. This principle of "eternal progression" is a stunningly unbiblical doctrine that sets Mormonism outside the boundaries of historic Christianity. At the same time, it raises questions, not only about God, but about the Son of God: Who is Jesus? Where did He come from? Why and how did He become human?

The doctrine of the Incarnation – God becoming a human being in Jesus of Nazareth – is central to Christianity.

Get it wrong and many other non-negotiable doctrines of the Christian faith quickly veer into counterfeit territory.

As we explore the Incarnation from a biblical perspective, it may help to compare Snow's "revelation" with the following orthodox statement from Christian author C.S. Lewis in *Mere Christianity*: "The Son of God became a man to enable men to become sons of God."[3]

The Incarnation Defined

The term "incarnation" is of Latin origin and literally means "enfleshment" or "embodiment." A Greek equivalent is found in Scripture: *en sarki [sarx]*. For example, John 1:14 reads: "The Word became flesh (*sarx egeneto*)." Simply put, the Incarnation means the eternal Son of God took on human flesh in the person of Jesus of Nazareth. As such, Jesus Christ is one person in two natures: divine and human.

The importance of this truth should not be overlooked. If Jesus is not divine, He cannot be the Christ; if He is not human, He cannot be our Savior.

Kenneth Samples writes, "This truth sets Christianity apart from all other religions of the world (including the monotheistic faiths of Judaism and Islam), for it is unique to Christianity to discover a God who takes the initiative to become flesh in order to redeem sinful human beings."[4]

As Christianity spread in the early decades of the church, it encountered competing views of God in paganism. And it wrestled with false teachings that assaulted the church from within. So, it became necessary to articulate a clear view of God as triune, and of Jesus as the God-Man – views consistent with the teaching of the apostles and the writings of the New Testament.

One of the most important statements on the Incarnation is the Creed of Chalcedon (AD 451). All Christendom – Roman Catholic, Eastern Orthodox, and Protestant – affirms the Chalcedonian formula that Jesus Christ is both God and man.

The creed says, in part: "We all with one voice confess our Lord Jesus Christ to be one and the same Son, perfect in divinity and humanity, truly God and truly human, consisting of a rational soul and a body, being of one substance with the Father in relation to his divinity, and being of one substance with us in relation to his humanity, and is like us in all things apart from sin."[5]

This means Jesus is not a god who only appeared to be human, as the Docetics taught; a mere man born of Mary and Joseph, as the Ebionites claimed; or the first and greatest creation of God, as the Arians believed (and Jehovah's Witnesses proclaim today). Rather, Jesus is the God-Man, one person with two distinct but undivided natures, divine and human. As Wayne Grudem summarizes, "Jesus Christ was fully God and fully man in one person, and will be so forever."[6]

The doctrine of the Incarnation flows naturally from a biblical understanding of the Trinity. Historic Christianity affirms belief in one infinitely perfect, eternal, and personal God, the transcendent Creator and sovereign Sustainer of the universe. This one God is triune, existing eternally and simultaneously as three distinct, but not separate, persons: Father, Son, and Holy Spirit.

In this light, Jesus clearly may be seen as the eternal Son of God who, in the Incarnation, set aside His privileged position at the Father's right hand (but not His deity) in order to become a sinless human who rescued us from sin by becoming sin for us on the cross (2 Cor. 5:21).

The Hypostatic Union

If Jesus is fully divine and fully human, how are we to understand the way in which these two natures work together?

At times, Jesus exhibits the fullness of deity – demonstrating His sovereign control over nature, forgiving sins, receiving worship, and knowing the thoughts of human beings. But He also displays the full range of humanity – getting hungry, growing tired, and, occasionally, not knowing certain things such as the time of His return.

So, when Jesus embarks on His earthly ministry, is He partly divine and partly human? Does He toggle back and forth between deity and humanity? Or is He simply an extraordinary human being who exhibits divine powers?

The message of the Incarnation is that the eternal Son of God became flesh – that is, He added sinless humanity to His deity, never relinquishing His deity or abandoning His humanity. This is sometimes explained by the term *hypostatic union* (from the Greek *hypostasis*, meaning "person"). This refers to the union of Jesus' two distinct natures in one person, without dividing the person or confounding His natures. Christ is one in substance with the Father in regard to His divine nature, and one in substance with humanity in regard to His human nature. The two natures unite perfectly in the one person of Jesus Christ.

As one author puts it, "Philosophically speaking, as the God-man, Jesus Christ is two 'whats' (i.e., a divine 'what' or nature and a human 'what' or nature) and one 'who' (i.e., a single 'person' or 'self')."[7]

Kenosis

In Philippians 2:7, Paul writes that Jesus "emptied himself by assuming the form of a servant, taking on the likeness of humanity." The Greek term for "emptied himself" (*ekenosen*) gives rise to *kenosis*, an attempt to explain how the two natures of Christ relate in the Incarnation.

A prominent heretical view of *kenosis* is that in order for Jesus to be human, He must shed certain attributes such as omnipotence, omniscience, or omnipresence. The phrase "emptied himself," it is argued, means that Jesus laid aside His divine attributes. Therefore, the incarnate Christ was something less than God.

A more biblically faithful view is that instead of stripping Himself of divine attributes, Jesus retained them in His divine nature. But in union with His human nature, He may have voluntarily chosen not to exercise certain attributes of His deity. Proponents of this view understand Philippians 2:7 not as undermining the deity of Christ, but expressing the surrender of the status and privileges He enjoyed in heaven. Put another way, Jesus surrendered His divine glory, not His divine power.[8]

TEN TRUTHS ABOUT THE INCARNATION

So far in this chapter, we have sought to establish that the Incarnation means the eternal Son of God took on human flesh in the person of Jesus of Nazareth. As such, Jesus is one person in two distinct but undivided natures: human and divine. In addition, we've explored how these two natures work together as the eternal Son of God adds sinless humanity to His deity via the miracle of the virgin birth.

Now, it may prove helpful to summarize essential truths about the Incarnation. These truths help us form a framework for better understanding the person and work of Christ. They also help establish a foundation for exploring the thornier issues related to the Incarnation.

The following ten truths are drawn from a number of sources, including the systematic theologies of Wayne Grudem, Charles Hodge, and Lewis Berkhof, and are summarized in *God Among Sages* by Kenneth Samples.

   1. Jesus Christ is one person possessing two distinct natures: a completely divine nature and a

completely human nature. Thus, Jesus of Nazareth may rightly be called the God-Man.

2. Christ is the same person both before and after the Incarnation. As the writer of Hebrews notes, He is the same "yesterday, today, and forever" (Heb. 13:8). The difference is that before the Incarnation, Jesus had but one nature (divine). In the Incarnation, He added a human nature, one that exists together with the original divine nature, which did not and will not disappear.

3. Through His divine nature, Jesus is God the Son, the second person of the Trinity, who shares the one divine essence fully and equally with the Father and the Holy Spirit. For example, when Jesus declares, "I and the Father are one," He clearly means one in essence, not just purpose. The unbelieving Jews who hear these words get the meaning, for they seek to stone Him for blasphemy (John 10:30-33).

4. Through His human nature, Jesus possesses and exhibits all the essential attributes of a true human being. He gets tired, hungry, and thirsty. He feels pain, experiences abandonment, and dies.

5. Jesus, as one person, retains all the attributes of both natures. For example, through His divine nature, He is omniscient, while simultaneously and voluntarily, through His human nature, He experiences a temporary lack of knowledge.

6. The union of Jesus' two natures is a true and personal union. In other words, it is not simply the indwelling of the divine presence in a human being, as is the case with Christians whom the Holy Spirit indwells. Rather, in Jesus, the divine and the human come together in one person.

7. The two natures form a perfect, complementary union. The human nature of Jesus is never without the divine nature, nor the divine without the human. To deny the deity of Christ at any point in eternity is to undermine His eternal existence as the sovereign Creator. To deny the full humanity of Jesus at any point after His miraculous conception in a virgin's womb is to refuse His necessary sacrifice on our behalf as the Word who became flesh (John 1:14).
8. Jesus' two natures – divine and human – are distinct and inseparably united in one person. The two natures retain their own attributes or qualities and thus are not mixed together.
9. The human nature is not deified – that is, Jesus' humanity does not become divine – and the divine nature does not suffer human limitations.
10. The word "nature" refers to essence or substance, and these two natures are inseparable, unmixed, and unchanged.[9]

These essential truths help us better understand the *hypostatic union*. They also assist us in separating biblical truth about the Incarnation from numerous heretical views that emerged early in Christian history, many of which continue today. We survey a variety of these false views later in this chapter. But first, it's important to examine key passages of Scripture about the Incarnation.

KEY PASSAGES ABOUT THE INCARNATION

Let's look briefly at six key passages of Scripture that help us understand what it means when the apostle John writes, "The Word became flesh" (John 1:14).

John 1:14 – "The Word became flesh and dwelt among

us. We observed his glory, the glory as the one and only Son from the Father, full of grace and truth."

The eternal Son of God always had a divine nature. He is with God in the beginning, and John makes it clear that Jesus was (and is) God (John 1:1). In the Incarnation, Jesus adds a real human nature and thus becomes the God-Man.

The word "dwelt" may be translated "tabernacled." Just as the divine presence is with ancient Israelites in the pillar of cloud and fire, as well as in the tabernacle and the temple, Yahweh now manifests Himself in the person of Jesus Christ.

Romans 1:3-4 – "concerning his Son, Jesus Christ our Lord, who was a descendant of David according to the flesh and was appointed to be the powerful Son of God according to the Spirit of holiness by the resurrection of the dead."

Paul recognizes Jesus' humanity through His ancestry as a descendant of King David. His divine nature as the unique Son of God, however, is proven through His miraculous resurrection from the dead.

Romans 9:5 – "The ancestors are theirs [the Israelites], and from them, by physical descent, came the Christ, who is God over all, praised forever. Amen."

Jesus' human nature is linked to His Jewish lineage, and His divine nature makes Him "God over all."

A few translations try to soften this clear statement of deity. The Contemporary English Version, for example, renders it, "I pray that God, who rules over all, will be praised forever!" However, contextually, this reference to "God over all" applies to the person of Christ and is not a separate praise of God.[10]

Philippians 2:5-7 – "Adopt the same attitude as that of Christ Jesus, who, existing in the form of God, did not consider equality with God as something to be exploited. Instead he emptied himself by assuming the form of a servant, taking on the likeness of humanity."

This passage reflects a primitive Christian hymn. From all

eternity, Jesus is of the same essence as God and thus is God. Even though Jesus possesses the nature and prerogatives of deity in eternity past, He does not cling to His privileged position at the Father's right hand. Rather, He humbles Himself, adding sinless humanity to His deity and thus becoming the God-Man.

Colossians 2:9 – "For the entire fullness of God's nature dwells bodily in Christ." As the NIV renders it, "For in Christ all the fullness of the Deity lives in bodily form."

In this passage, the apostle Paul responds to heretical views that later find their place in Gnosticism – namely, the categorical denial that Christ has come in the flesh. Paul emphatically states that Jesus is full divinity wrapped in human skin. The Incarnation is central to Paul's writings here and elsewhere.

1 John 4:2 – "This is how you know the Spirit of God: Every spirit that confesses that Jesus Christ has come in the flesh is from God ..."

The apostle John counters first-century Docetics, a heretical group that embraces the deity of Christ but denies His humanity, arguing that Jesus only appears to be human (from the Greek *dokeo*, "to seem"). John makes Christ in the flesh a true test of Christian orthodoxy, arguing that every true "spirit" – a person claiming divine gifting for service – upholds the doctrine of the God-Man.

These verses illustrate the significance of the Incarnation. As theologian Gerald Bray writes, "The Son of God, eternally begotten of the Father and fully equal to him in every respect, became a man so that he could unite us to himself, pay the price for our sins, and bring us back to God."[11]

INCARNATIONAL HERESIES

As we complete our examination of the Incarnation, it's important to identify a number of heretical views that have plagued Christianity throughout its history. The church has effectively countered some of these heresies, while others continue to rear their ugly heads and cause people who sincerely seek the truth to embrace "another Jesus" (2 Cor. 11:4).

Kenneth Samples highlights eight historical heresies with respect to the Incarnation:

Docetism. This was an early form of Gnosticism, a heresy that threatened the fledgling church throughout its first three centuries. Docetism advanced a type of dualism, expressing the belief that spirit is good and matter is evil.

Docetics argued that Jesus only appeared to be human. In fact, their name comes from the Greek word *dokeo*, which means "to seem." They asserted that Jesus had a "phantom-like body."

Docetism denied the true humanity of Jesus, which undermined the reality of His death on the cross, burial, and physical resurrection – all necessary elements in the gospel message. The apostle John confronted Docetism in 1 John 4:1-3.

Ebionism. This was a Jewish sect that denied the deity of Christ. Ebionites believed Jesus to be a mere man, a natural son of Mary and Joseph. While they honored Jesus as a prophet, they failed to acknowledge His true identity as the eternal Son of God who was born of a virgin.

Arianism. Arius of Alexandria (AD 256-336) was a priest who argued that Jesus was the first and greatest creation of God. Thus, he denied Jesus' true deity. This heretical view spread widely and nearly wrecked the early church until Athanasius successfully countered it and the Council of Nicaea (AD 325) first condemned it.

Arianism is alive and well today in counterfeit Christian organizations like the Watch Tower Bible and Tract Society (Jehovah's Witnesses), which holds that Jesus is the first of Jehovah's created beings, namely, Michael the archangel.

Apollinarianism. Apollinaris was a fourth-century

bishop of Laodicea who taught that Jesus' humanity was restricted to His physical body. In other words, Jesus did not have a human soul. Rather, the divine *Logos* (Word) took the place of the immaterial part of Jesus of Nazareth.

In effect, while Apollinaris affirmed the Incarnation, he wrongly defined it and thus rejected the full humanity of the Son of Man. The First Council of Constantinople (AD 381) condemned Apollinarianism as heresy.

Nestorianism. This view affirmed both Christ's deity and His humanity but stressed the distinctiveness of the two natures. Jesus was seen as two persons in two natures rather than as one person in two natures.

Nestorians saw the union of Christ's two natures as moral, or sympathetic, rather than as a real, personal union. The Council of Ephesus (AD 431) condemned this as heresy.

Eutychianism. Eutyches (AD 378-454) was a leader of the Eastern Church at Constantinople. He taught that Jesus had a single nature that was neither divine nor human. Rather, it was a third substance that mixed the divine and the human.

In essence, Eutychianism over-emphasized the unity of Jesus' divine and human natures. The Council of Chalcedon (AD 451) and the Third Council of Constantinople (AD 680) condemned this view as heretical.

Monophysitism. This view, which the Third Council of Constantinople declared heretical, contended that Jesus had only one nature. Proponents of this view usually argued that Christ's human nature was absorbed into His divine nature.

Monothelitism. The Third Council of Constantinople also condemned this view as heretical. Essentially, it taught that Christ had only one will. This is in contrast to the orthodox position, which holds that because Jesus had two natures, He also had two wills – divine and human – although the human will always conformed to the divine will.[12]

These heretical views illustrate at least two characteristics of the church's effort to understand the Incarnation. First, the early church struggled to fully comprehend the teaching of Jesus and the apostles about what it meant for the Word to become flesh (John 1:14). Second, Satan was quick to sow tares in the wheat field of God's kingdom.

SUMMARY

While Jesus shares all the divine attributes of God the Father and the Holy Spirit (Col. 2:9), He is unique among the persons of the Godhead in that only He has taken on human flesh. That is so He could experience the full range of humanity, including every form of temptation, on our behalf. Having lived a sinless life, He laid it down for us on the cross, satisfying the wrath of God for our sins and extending to us the unmerited offer of forgiveness and everlasting life. Truly, the God-Man is the Lamb of God who takes away the sin of the world (John 1:29).

It is difficult to wrap our finite minds around the mystery of the Incarnation. Yet this much is clear: Sinful, fallen, and finite people can never repay the debt owed a holy, transcendent, and eternal God. So, in the wake of Adam's sin, the triune God unveils a plan to rescue His wretched creatures from sin and its consequences.

The key is God becoming a man in the person of Jesus of Nazareth. This seemingly unremarkable human being (Isa. 53:2), born in inglorious surroundings (Luke 2:7), raised in an unexceptional village (John 1:46), learning His family's undistinguished craft (Matt. 13:55), performs the most incredible feat. While identifying with fallen sinners, and being tempted in every conceivable way, Jesus fulfills every jot and tittle of God's perfect law. Then, He offers His life to God the Father as payment for the sins of humans who, from the start, have proven unable and unwilling to pay the debt themselves.

And consider this stunning truth: While Jesus is on earth

for only thirty-odd years, He retains His humanity forever. Having finished the work the Father sent Him to do, He rises physically from the dead and ascends physically into heaven, where today He remains seated at the Father's right hand, interceding on our behalf until the Father sends Him back to earth to judge, rule, and purge the created order of sin once and for all. At no time does Jesus forsake the marks of His crucifixion or the flesh and bones of His humanity. When He returns, "every eye will see him, even those who pierced him" (Rev. 1:7, cf. Zech. 12:10). For all eternity, Jesus continues as the God-Man – God with us and, forevermore, one of us.

In a classic sermon on Isaiah 53:3, Charles Spurgeon urges us to consider the wonder of the divine becoming human:

> We can never meditate too much upon Christ's blessed person as God and as man. Let us reflect that He who is here called a man was certainly "very God of very God." "A man," and "a man of sorrows," and yet at the same time, "God over all, blessed forever." He who was "despised and rejected of men" was beloved and adored by angels. And He, from whom men hid their faces in contempt, was worshipped by cherubim and seraphim. This is the great mystery of godliness. God was "manifest in the flesh." He who was God, and was in the beginning with God, was made flesh and dwelt among us. The Highest stooped to become the lowest; the Greatest took His place among the least. Strange, and needing all our faith to grasp it, yet it is true that He who sat upon the well of Sychar, and said, "Give Me to drink," was none other than He who dug the channels of the ocean, and poured into them the floods. Son of Mary, You are also Son of Jehovah! Man of the substance of Your mother, You are also essential Deity! We worship You this day in spirit and in truth![13]

REVIEW

1. The Bible is clear that Jesus is the God-Man. That is, two thousand years ago, the eternal Son of God added sinless _____ to His deity through the _____ birth and thus became the only person in history with two natures: _____ and human. This is the doctrine of the _____.

2. The importance of the Incarnation should not be overlooked. If Jesus is not divine, He cannot be the _____; if He is not human, He cannot be our _____. This truth sets Christianity apart from all other religions of the world, including the monotheistic faiths of Judaism and _____.

3. Two terms are sometimes used to help us better understand the Incarnation:

(a) *Hypostatic union* refers to the union of Jesus' two distinct _____ in one person, without dividing the person or confounding His natures. Christ is one in substance with the _____ in regard to His divine nature, and one in substance with _____ in regard to His human nature.

(b) *Kenosis* refers to the manner in which Jesus "emptied himself by assuming the form of a servant, taking on the _____ of humanity" (Phil. 2:7). That is, instead of stripping Himself of divine attributes, Jesus retained them in His divine _____. But in union with His human nature, He may have voluntarily chosen not to _____ certain attributes of

His deity. Put another way, Jesus surrendered His divine glory, not His divine _____.

4. Complete the following passages about the Incarnation:

(a) John 1:14 – "The Word became _____ and dwelt among us …"

(b) Romans 1:3-4 – "concerning his Son, Jesus Christ our Lord, who was a descendant of _____ according to the flesh and was appointed to be the powerful _____ of God according to the Spirit of holiness by the _____ of the dead."

(c) Romans 9:5 – "The ancestors are theirs [the Israelites], and from them, by physical descent, came the Christ, who is _____ over all, praised forever. Amen."

(d) Philippians 2:5-7 – "Adopt the same attitude as that of Christ Jesus, who, existing in the _____ of God, did not consider equality with God as something to be exploited. Instead, He _____ himself by assuming the form of a servant, taking on the likeness of humanity."

(e) Colossians 2:9 – "For the entire fullness of God's _____ dwells bodily in Christ."

(f) 1 John 4:2 – "This is how you know the _____ of God: Every spirit that confesses that Jesus Christ has come in the _____ is from God …"

5. A number of heretical views about Jesus have plagued the church throughout its history. Among these false views is

Docetism, an early form of _____, which advanced a type of dualism, expressing the belief that spirit is good and _____ is evil. Docetics argued that Jesus only _____ to be human.

THINK

Questions for personal or group study

1. How would you answer the following questions:

   - If Jesus is God, and if God knows everything, why does Jesus say in Mark 13:32 that He doesn't know the day or hour of His return?
   - If Jesus is divine, why do the Gospels show Him getting tired, thirsty, and hungry?
   - How can Jesus say in John 10:30 that He and the Father are one, and then insist in John 14:28 that the Father is greater than He is?
   - If Jesus truly is divine, and He died on the cross, how is it possible for God to die?

2. How would you explain the importance of the Incarnation to someone who believes Jesus was a good man, but only a man? Specifically, think about why it's essential to our salvation that God became flesh in Jesus of Nazareth.

3. What's wrong with the following statements about the Incarnation:

(a) Jesus was a "divine being" – a god, if you will – but not Jehovah.

(b) Jesus was a great messenger of God. He was born of a

virgin, performed miracles, and led a sinless life. But he was only a man delivering God's message.

(c) When Jesus left heaven and came to earth, He temporarily set aside His deity to become a man. When He ascended into heaven after His resurrection, He reclaimed His deity.

(d) In the Incarnation, Jesus became a mix of the divine and the human. That is, He was partly God and partly man.

(e) Jesus' earthly life was like a toggle switch. He could turn on and off His deity.

4. Why is it important that Jesus retains His complete humanity forever? If He finished the work that God the Father sent Him to do on earth, why does He have to keep His human body now that He's back in heaven?

5. Provide a brief description of the following heresies:

Docetism

_____

_____

_____

Arianism

_____

_____

Nestorianism

Monophysitism

CHAPTER EIGHT

The Holy Spirit is God

In some ways, the Holy Spirit is the neglected, if not forgotten, member of the Trinity. The biblical doctrines of foreknowledge, election, predestination, and adoption awaken us to the eternal love of God the Father. Through the Incarnation, the second person of the triune Godhead becomes flesh and pitches His tent with us (John 1:14). He experiences in full measure what it means to be human, including facing temptation – yet without sinning so that He may clothe us in God's righteousness (2 Cor. 5:21). Christians are said to have a personal relationship with Jesus Christ and to be the adopted sons and daughters of God the Father.

But where is the Holy Spirit in all of this? As we see in upcoming chapters about creation, salvation, and Scripture, none of the persons of the Godhead acts alone. As such, the Holy Spirit is a co-equal and co-eternal partner in all of the Trinity's work. So, it's important for us to understand how thoroughly the Bible depicts both the personhood and deity of the Holy Spirit. We focus first on the Spirit as a person, for without personhood the Spirit cannot be divine. Next, we show from Scripture how this person possesses all the attributes of deity found in both the Father and the Son.

The world's major religions recognize the Holy Spirit, as do the most popular forms of counterfeit Christianity, yet they define the Spirit in a way that denies His personhood, His deity, or both. For example, Islam depicts the Holy Spirit as none other than the angel Gabriel, who delivered the Qur'an to the prophet Mohammad. Jehovah's Witnesses deny both the personhood and the deity of the Holy Spirit, referring to Him as "holy spirit" and likening Him to a powerful, impersonal force. And Latter-day Saints distinguish between the Holy Ghost, who is personal, and the Holy Spirit, which (sometimes) is not. As we see in this chapter, these views do not align with Scripture.

THE PERSONALITY OF THE HOLY SPIRIT

One way the Jehovah's Witnesses' New World Translation (NWT) seeks to undermine the Trinity is by consistently rendering the name "Holy Spirit" as the inanimate "holy spirit." The unnamed translators of the NWT often omit the article "the," which results in stilted verses such as:

Matthew 1:18 - Mary, the mother of Jesus, "was found to be pregnant by holy spirit [or 'active force'] ..."

Matthew 3:11 - "That one [Jesus] will baptize you with holy spirit ..."

Luke 1:15 - John the Baptist "will be filled with holy spirit even from before birth."

As James White notes, "Their intention is clear: the Watchtower society denies that the Holy Spirit is a person, hence, they desire their 'translation' of the Bible to communicate the idea that the Holy Spirit is an 'it,' a force or power."[1]

The Watch Tower argues that the phrase "Holy Spirit" in Greek is in the neuter gender, and it is. But Greek genders do not necessarily indicate personality. Inanimate objects can have masculine and feminine genders, and personal beings can have the neuter gender.

A better way to determine whether the Holy Spirit is personal is the same way we seek to understand whether the Father and Son are personal. That is, does the Holy Spirit offer evidence of personhood? Does He speak, use personal pronouns, have a will, and so on? The answer, of course, is a resounding yes.

Personal Pronouns

One of the clearest demonstrations of the Holy Spirit's personality is His use of personal pronouns in reference to Himself. Two examples make this plain:

Acts 10:19-20 – "While Peter was thinking about the vision, the Spirit told him, 'Three men are here looking for you. Get up, go downstairs, and go with them with no doubts at all, because *I* have sent them'" (emphasis added).

Acts 13:1-2 – "Now in the church at Antioch there were prophets and teachers: Barnabas, Simeon who was called Niger, Lucius of Cyrene, Manaen, a close friend of Herod the tetrarch, and Saul. As they were worshiping the Lord and fasting, the Holy Spirit said, 'Set apart for *me* Barnabas and Saul for the work to which *I* have called them'" (emphasis added).

Note that the Holy Spirit speaks personally to Peter as well as to believers in the Antioch church. He sends people to fetch Peter, and He calls Barnabas and Saul to mission work. And He uses personal pronouns. These are actions of a sentient being, not an impersonal force.

Jesus also uses personal pronouns to speak of the coming Holy Spirit, telling His followers, "When the Counselor comes, the one I will send to you from the Father – the Spirit of truth who proceeds from the Father – *he* will testify about me" (John 15:26, emphasis added).

Later, Jesus again informs His disciples, "When the Spirit of truth comes, *he* will guide you into all the truth. For he will not speak on *his* own, but he will speak whatever he hears. He will also declare to you what is to come. *He* will glorify me, because he will take from what is mine and declare it to you" (John 16:13-14, emphasis added where the Greek uses pronouns; the CSB and other translations add pronouns for clarity).

According to Jesus, the Holy Spirit arrives, guides, discerns the truth, hears and speaks, discloses future events, testifies about Jesus, and glorifies Him – all demonstrations of personhood.

Personal Activities

Now, let's consider several passages of Scripture that describe the Holy Spirit's personal activities. We may see that the Spirit:

Speaks. In the last recorded words of King David, he claims to speak for God under the inspiration of the Holy Spirit: "The Spirit of the Lord spoke through me, his word was on my tongue" (2 Sam. 23:2).

In Luke's account of the Ethiopian official's conversion, he notes, "The Spirit told Philip, 'Go and join that chariot'" (Acts 8:29). After Philip proclaims the gospel to the official and baptizes him, "the Spirit of the Lord carried Philip away" until Philip is found in Azotus. From there, he works his way to Caesarea, preaching from town to town, no doubt still under the Spirit's direction (vv. 39-40).

Counsels. Jesus assures His followers that after His return to heaven, He will send another Counselor (Greek *parakletos* – advocate) like Himself. The Spirit will not only be with them, but *in* them (John 14:16-17).

Prophesies. The Spirit causes Balaam, an evil prophet for hire, to prophesy only good things for Israel: "When Balaam looked up and saw Israel encamped tribe by tribe, the Spirit of God came on him, and he proclaimed his poem:

The oracle of Balaam son of Beor,
the oracle of the man whose eyes are opened,
the oracle of one who hears the sayings of God,
who sees a vision from the Almighty,
who falls into a trance with his eyes uncovered ..."
(Num. 24:2-4).

Reveals future events. When a prophet named Agabus visits Paul in Philip's home in Caesarea, he takes Paul's belt, ties his own feet and hands with it, and says, "This is what the Holy Spirit says: 'In this way the Jews in Jerusalem will bind the man who owns this belt and deliver him over to the Gentiles'" (Acts 21:11).

Chooses and empowers. The Spirit installs and enables the judges of Israel, such as Othniel: "The Israelites cried out to the Lord. So the Lord raised up Othniel son of Kenaz, Caleb's youngest brother, as a deliverer to save the Israelites. The Spirit of the Lord came on him, and he judged Israel ..." (Judg. 3:9-10).

Other Old Testament passages reveal the work of the Spirit in choosing and empowering people (see, for example, Exod. 31:1-11; Isa. 11:2; 44:3-5;). These verses show how closely related the concept of the Holy Spirit is to the very being of God.

Testifies. Paul writes, "The Spirit himself testifies together with our spirit that we are God's children, and if children, also heirs – heirs of God and coheirs with Christ – if indeed we suffer with him so that we may also be glorified with him." (Rom. 8:16-17).

Note that the Spirit, Father, and Son work together in our adoption as God's children. In another passage, Jesus tells His followers that the coming Holy Spirit will testify about Him: "When the Counselor comes, the one I will send to you from the Father — the Spirit of truth who proceeds from the Father — he will testify about me" (John 15:26).

Commenting about Jesus' teaching on the Holy Spirit in John 14-16, Freddy Davis writes, "Jesus does not call the Holy Spirit 'It,' nor does He imply that the Spirit is impersonal. In fact Jesus emphasizes both the divine nature and the personal dimension of the Holy Spirit."[2]

Confirms our adoption into God's family. The apostle Paul writes to the Galatians, "And because you are sons, God sent the Spirit of his Son into our hearts, crying, '*Abba*, Father!' So you are no longer a slave but a son, and if a son, then God has made you an heir" (Gal. 4:6-7). Like Jesus in the Garden of Gethsemane (Mark 14:36), the Holy Spirit refers to the Father as *Abba*, or Papa. As adopted sons and daughters of God, we may do the same.

Intercedes on our behalf. Paul explains that "the Spirit also helps us in our weakness, because we do not know what to pray for as we should, but the Spirit himself intercedes for us with unspoken groanings. And he who searches our hearts knows the mind of the Spirit, because he intercedes for the saints according to the will of God" (Rom. 8:26-27). Only a person may help another person by interceding on his or her behalf.

Knows God's thoughts. To the Corinthians, Paul writes, "Now God has revealed these things to us by the Spirit, since the Spirit searches everything, even the depths of God. For who knows a person's thoughts except his spirit within him? In the same way, no one knows the thoughts of God except the Spirit of God" (1 Cor. 2:10-11). The apostle goes on to describe how the Spirit explains "spiritual things to spiritual people" (v. 13).

Appoints overseers to shepherd the church. Paul tells the Ephesian elders, "Be on guard for yourselves and for all the flock of which the Holy Spirit has appointed you as overseers, to shepherd the church of God, which he purchased with his own blood" (Acts 20:28).

Distributes spiritual gifts. In writing to the

Corinthians about spiritual gifts, Paul depicts all three members of the Godhead working together, emphasizing that "God produces each gift in each person" (1 Cor. 12:6). After a partial listing of these gifts, Paul concludes, "One and the same Spirit is active in all these, distributing to each person as he wills" (v. 11).

Bestows talents. The Lord fills Bezalel "with God's Spirit, with wisdom, understanding, and ability in every craft to design artistic works in gold, silver, and bronze, to cut gemstones for mounting, and to carve wood for work in every craft" (Exod. 31:2-5).

Is present with God's people. In his gut-wrenching confession of sin, David implores the Lord, "Do not banish me from your presence or take your Holy Spirit from me" (Ps. 51:11).

Leads. To the Romans, Paul writes, "because if you live according to the flesh, you are going to die. But if by the Spirit you put to death the deeds of the body, you will live. For all those led by God's Spirit are God's sons" (Rom. 8:13-14). Only a person leads purposefully, and only a person engages in the adoption of another person.

Forbids and allows. Paul and Timothy "went through the region of Phrygia and Galatia; they had been forbidden by the Holy Spirit to speak the word in Asia. When they came to Mysia, they tried to go into Bithynia, but the Spirit of Jesus did not allow them" (Acts 16:6-7). Only a person directs others by forbidding and allowing.

May be blasphemed. When certain Pharisees accuse Jesus of casting out demons by the power of Satan, Jesus responds that He drives out demons by the Spirit of God (Matt. 12:24-28). He continues, "Therefore, I tell you, people will be forgiven every sin and blasphemy, but the blasphemy against the Spirit will not be forgiven" (v. 31; see also Mark 3:28-29).

May be grieved. Paul warns the Ephesians, "And don't

grieve God's Holy Spirit. You were sealed by him for the day of redemption" (Eph. 4:30). And the prophet Isaiah reminds the house of Israel of its shameful response to the Lord's goodness: "But they rebelled and grieved his Holy Spirit. So he became their enemy and fought against them. Then he remembered the days of the past, the days of Moses and his people. Where is he who brought them out of the sea with the shepherds of his flock? Where is he who put his Holy Spirit among the flock?" (Isa. 63:10-11).

Only a person may be grieved, and only a person makes the conscious choice to provide security for another person.

May be insulted. The writer of Hebrews warns his readers of the danger of deliberate sin: "Anyone who disregarded the law of Moses died without mercy, based on the testimony of two or three witnesses. How much worse punishment do you think one will deserve who has trampled on the Son of God, who has regarded as profane the blood of the covenant by which he was sanctified, and who has insulted the Spirit of grace?" (Heb. 10:28-29).

Imparts new life. Jesus tells Nicodemus of the regenerating work of the Holy Spirit: "Truly I tell you, unless someone is born of water and the Spirit, he cannot enter the kingdom of God. Whatever is born of the flesh is flesh, and whatever is born of the Spirit is spirit. Do not be amazed that I told you that you must be born again. The wind blows where it pleases, and you hear its sound, but you don't know where it comes from or where it is going. So it is with everyone born of the Spirit" (John 3:5-8).

Other passages could be cited, but these are sufficient to demonstrate the personality of the Holy Spirit.

THE DEITY OF THE HOLY SPIRIT

So far, we have examined the biblical evidence for the personhood of the Holy Spirit; that is, the Spirit is a *He*, not an *it*.

Once the Spirit's personality is established, His deity is a logical, and biblically faithful, next step. So, what do we see the Spirit doing that only God can do?

For starters, the Holy Spirit *creates*. Genesis 1:2 records, "Now the earth was formless and empty, darkness covered the surface of the watery depths, and the Spirit of God was hovering over the surface of the waters." The Hebrew verb translated "was hovering," used also in Deuteronomy 32:11, suggests that the Spirit of God was watching over His creation just as a bird watches over its young.[3] Further, creatures come into being when God sends His Spirit (Ps. 104:30).

In addition, the Spirit *demonstrates omniscience and omnipresence*, displaying qualities that establish Him as co-equal and co-eternal with the Father and the Son. Of the Spirit's omniscience, Paul writes, "Now God has revealed these things to us by the Spirit, since the Spirit searches everything, even the depths of God. For who knows a person's thoughts except his spirit within him? In the same way, no one knows the thoughts of God except the Spirit of God" (1 Cor. 2:10-11). Of omnipresence, the psalmist asks, "Where can I go to escape your Spirit? Where can I flee from your presence? If I go up to heaven, you are there; if I make my bed in Sheol, you are there" (Ps. 139:7-8).

What's more, the Spirit *shares a divine name*, symbolic of divine presence, with the other members of the triune Godhead. Before Jesus ascends into heaven, He commands His followers, "Go, therefore, and make disciples of all nations, baptizing them in the name of the Father and of the Son and of the Holy Spirit" (Matt. 28:19).

Perhaps the clearest passage that illustrates both the personality and deity of the Holy Spirit is found in Acts 5. After Ananias and Sapphira fraudulently claim to have given the full proceeds of a land sale to the church, Peter confronts Ananias, asking, "[W]hy has Satan filled your heart to lie to the Holy Spirit and keep back part of the proceeds of the land? Wasn't it yours while you possessed it? And after it was sold, wasn't it at your disposal? Why is it that you planned this thing in your heart? You have not lied to people but to God" (vv. 3-4).

To whom did Ananias lie: to the Holy Spirit, or to God? The answer, of course, is that Ananias lied to both. To lie to the Holy Spirit is to lie to God since the Spirit occupies an equal place in the Trinity with the Father and the Son.

Consider what the apostle Paul writes to the Corinthians in two related passages. First, in 1 Corinthians 3:16-17, he asks, "Don't you yourselves know that you are God's temple and that the Spirit of God lives in you? If anyone destroys God's temple, God will destroy him; for God's temple is holy, and that is what you are."

Paul uses similar language three chapters later: "Don't you know that your body is a temple of the Holy Spirit who is in you, whom you have from God? You are not your own, for you were bought at a price. So glorify God with your body" (1 Cor. 6:19-20).

Put simply, when the Holy Spirit indwells us, God indwells us. By equating the phrase "God's temple" with "the temple of the Holy Spirit," Paul makes it clear that the Holy Spirit is God.

The writer of Hebrews contributes to this theme, stating that the Holy Spirit is eternal, an attribute of God: "For if the blood of goats and bulls and the ashes of a young cow, sprinkling those who are defiled, sanctify for the purification of the flesh, how much more will the blood of Christ, who through *the eternal Spirit* offered himself without blemish to God, cleanse our consciences from dead works so that we can serve the living God?" (Heb. 9:13-14, emphasis added).

Finally, Paul refers to the Spirit as "Lord," using the Greek word *kyrios*. This term is applied to other members of the Godhead in the New Testament, and it is the word used to translate the divine name *Yahweh* in the Septuagint, the Greek translation of the Old Testament. Paul writes, "Now the Lord is the Spirit, and where the Spirit of the Lord is, there is freedom. We all, with unveiled faces, are looking as in a mirror at the glory of the Lord and are being transformed into the same image from glory to glory; this is from the Lord who is the Spirit" (2 Cor. 3:17-18).

Divine Power

Additional evidence of the Spirit's deity comes in several passages that attest to His divine power:

Luke 1:35 – The angel Gabriel tells Mary, "The Holy Spirit will come upon you, and the power of the Most High will overshadow you. Therefore, the holy one to be born will be called the Son of God." The parallel sentence structure featuring "The Holy Spirit" and "the power of the Most High" indicates the divine power by which the Spirit brought about the miracle of Christ's conception in a virgin's womb.

John 16:8-11 – Jesus credits the Holy Spirit with the power to change human hearts. Specifically, the Spirit convicts unbelievers of sin, righteousness, and judgment. He also makes us spiritually alive through His work of regeneration (John 3:5-8; Titus 3:5).

Romans 8:11 – Paul notes, "And if the Spirit of him who raised Jesus from the dead lives in you, then he who raised Christ from the dead will also bring your mortal bodies to life through his Spirit who lives in you." The same Holy Spirit who raised Jesus from the dead dwells in our mortal bodies. He grants us new life now, and He guarantees physical resurrection for our mortal bodies in the future.

Romans 15:18-19 – Paul writes, "For I would not dare say anything except what Christ has accomplished through me by word and deed for the obedience of the Gentiles, by the power of miraculous signs and wonders, and by the power of God's Spirit."

AN INTIMATE RELATIONSHIP

Scripture reveals the relationship between the Holy Spirit and the other members of the Godhead. As one example, note how the synoptic Gospel writers report Jesus' promise to be with His followers when they face persecution:

Matthew 10:19-20 – "But when they hand you over, don't worry about how or what you are to speak. For you will be given what to say at that hour, because it isn't you speaking, but *the Spirit of your Father* is speaking through you" (emphasis added).

Mark 13:11 – "So when they arrest you and hand you over, don't worry beforehand what you will say, but say whatever is given to you at that time, for it isn't you speaking, but *the Holy Spirit*" (emphasis added).

Luke 21:14-15 – "Therefore make up your minds not to prepare your defense ahead of time, for *I [Jesus]* will give you such words and a wisdom that none of your adversaries will be able to resist or contradict" (emphasis added).

These accounts are not in conflict. Rather, they illustrate the inseparability of the divine persons of the Trinity. That is, the Father, Son, and Holy Spirit, while distinct persons within the Godhead, share the same divine essence and act in perfect harmony.

We further see this in the Lord's promise to be with His people: "Jesus answered, 'If anyone loves me, he will keep my word. My Father will love him, and we will come to him and make our home with him'" (John 14:23).

Jesus promises that both He and the Father will dwell with those who love Him and keep His word. But how is this possible? Because both the Father and the Son send the Holy Spirit. Jesus tells His disciples, "But the Counselor, the Holy Spirit, whom *the Father will send in my name*, will teach you all things and remind you of everything I have told you" (John 14:26; emphasis added).

In the next chapter, Jesus says, "When the Counselor comes, the one *I will send to you from the Father* – the Spirit of truth who proceeds from the Father – he will testify about me" (John 15:26; emphasis added).

Both the Father and Jesus send the Holy Spirit to dwell in the human spirits of the redeemed. Just as the full deity of the Godhead is expressed in bodily form in Jesus (Col. 2:9), so the full deity of the Trinity rests in the Holy Spirit, who resides in the temples of believers' bodies (1 Cor. 6:19).

The relationship of the three persons of the Trinity is so intimate that Paul describes the Holy Spirit as the Spirit of God and the Spirit of Christ within a single verse: "You, however, are not in the flesh, but in the Spirit, if indeed the Spirit of God lives in you. If anyone does not have the Spirit of Christ, he does not belong to him" (Rom. 8:9).

The fellowship that believers experience as a result of the indwelling Holy Spirit is a taste of the supernatural unity that has always existed among the members of the Trinity. Perhaps that's why Paul and other first-century Christians include all three persons of the Godhead in their praises: "The grace of the Lord Jesus Christ, and the love of God, and the fellowship of the Holy Spirit be with you all" (2 Cor. 13:13).

SUMMARY

The Bible is replete with references to the personality and deity of the Holy Spirit. A faithful rendering of God's Word leads us to the conclusion that the Holy Spirit is an equal partner with the Father and the Son in the Godhead. His role in creation, redemption, and the revealing of Scripture is distinct yet inseparable from the work of the other members of the Trinity. None of the divine persons of the Godhead acts alone.

While the Spirit in some ways is the most neglected member of the Trinity, Scripture shows Him to possess all the attributes of deity – eternality, omnipotence, omniscience, and omnipresence, to name a few – while simultaneously exhibiting all the traits of divine personality as the Creator of all and the Counselor to those who follow Jesus.

REVIEW

1. In some ways, the Holy Spirit is the neglected, if not forgotten, member of the _____. Yet the Bible tells us that the Spirit is co-equal and co-_____ with the Father and the Son. It's important for us to understand how thoroughly the Bible depicts the _____ and deity of the Holy Spirit.

2. One of the clearest demonstrations of the Holy Spirit's personality is His use of personal pronouns in reference to Himself. Consider the following passages of Scripture and fill in the blanks with the correct personal pronoun:

Acts 10:19-20 – "While Peter was thinking about the vision, the Spirit told him, 'Three men are here looking for you. Get up, go downstairs, and go with them with no doubts at all, because _____ have sent them.'"

Acts 13:1-2 – "Now in the church at _____ there were prophets and teachers: Barnabas, Simeon who was called Niger, Lucius of Cyrene, Manaen, a close friend of _____ the tetrarch, and Saul. As they were worshiping the Lord and fasting, the Holy Spirit said, 'Set apart for _____ Barnabas and Saul for the work to which _____ have called them.'"

3. In what personal activities does the Holy Spirit engage in the following Bible verses:

2 Samuel 23:2 – "The Spirit of the Lord _____ through me, his word was on my tongue."

Acts 20:28 – "Be on guard for yourselves and for all the flock of which the Holy Spirit has _____ you as overseers, to shepherd the church of God, which he purchased with his own blood."

Romans 8:16 – "The Spirit himself _____ together with our spirit that we are God's children …"

Ephesians 4:30 – "And don't _____ God's Holy Spirit. You were _____ by him for the day of redemption."

4. The Holy Spirit is a _____, not an *it*. Once the Spirit's personality is established, His _____ is a logical, and biblically faithful, next step.

5. Scripture reveals the deity of the Holy Spirit, in part, by showing Him doing things only God can do. For example, the Spirit _____ (Gen. 1:2); demonstrates omniscience (1 Cor. 2:10-11) and _____ (Ps. 139:7-8); and shares a divine _____ with the Father and the Son (Matt. 28:19).

THINK

Questions for personal or group study

1. The world's major religions recognize the Holy Spirit, as do the most popular forms of counterfeit Christianity, yet they define the Spirit in a way that either denies His personhood,

deity, or both. Who do Muslims say the Holy Spirit is? How do Jehovah's Witnesses depict "holy spirit"? And how do Latter-day Saints distinguish between the Holy Ghost and the Holy Spirit?

2. Could the Holy Spirit be an impersonal force and still be a member of the Trinity? Why or why not? Think of this another way: If the Holy Spirit is merely a divine force and not a person, can God still be triune?

3. How do the following passages of Scripture describe the personhood of the Holy Spirit:

John 15:26

_____

_____

_____

Acts 8:29

_____

_____

_____

Romans 8:26-27

_____

_____

1 Corinthians 12:1-11

Hebrews 10:28-29

4. How do the following verses reveal the deity of the Holy Spirit:

Genesis 1:2

Luke 1:35

Acts 5:1-4

Romans 15:18-19

1 Corinthians 3:16-17

5. Read Matthew 10:19-20; Mark 13:11; and Luke 21:14-15. How do these accounts of Jesus' promise to be with His followers illustrate the intimacy of the relationship between the Father, Son, and Holy Spirit?

CHAPTER NINE

The Trinity and Creation

The Bible begins with a simple yet profound statement: "In the beginning God created the heavens and the earth" (Gen. 1:1). As Moses tells the story of creation, he does not seek to prove the existence of God. The Israelites have experienced God's presence and power first-hand. This includes Moses' encounter with Yahweh at the burning bush; the Lord's miraculous victory over the false gods of Egypt; His thunderous giving of the law at Mt. Sinai; His visible presence in the pillar of cloud and fire; and His parting of the Jordan River to make way for a dramatic entrance into the Promised Land.

As we continue through Scripture, we see that other human authors presuppose God's existence as the eternal, all-powerful, all-knowing, everywhere-present Creator. In fact, the apostle Paul simply tells us that the creation speaks for itself concerning the existence of God. The observable earth and skies reveal a divine Designer, while a universally shared human conscience displays the transcendence of a moral Law Giver. Together, this evidence is so convincing that no one stands before God in final judgment with a valid defense for having rejected Him (see Rom. 1:18-32; 2:12-16).

But who is this God, the Creator of heaven and earth? Is He a monolithic, unknowable, unapproachable being who reveals His will but not Himself, as Muslims claim? Is He a singular divine person who creates a lesser god through whom all other things exist, as Jehovah's Witnesses confess? Is He a Heavenly Father who, as a member of a council of gods, organized our world as distinct from other worlds, as Latter-day Saints proclaim? Or is the God of Scripture one being who exists in triunity, fashioning the natural world out of nothing, and sustaining it – even in its fallen state – until it is purged of sin and restored to pristine innocence (see 2 Pet. 3:5-13; Rev. 21-22)?

Up to this point in our study, we have seen how the Bible reveals one true and living God, who exists as three distinct, but inseparable, co-equal, co-eternal persons: Father, Son, and Holy Spirit. Did these three persons work together to create everything that exists, even the unseen realm of angelic beings? The answer is yes. In fact, throughout the Old Testament, God scolds the idols the Israelites worship precisely because these idols cannot claim to have created the world (see Jer. 10:10-11). Although Scripture most clearly depicts God the Father as Creator, we may see that He never acts independently. Rather, He works in concert with the Son and the Holy Spirit. This includes the Godhead's collaborative work of creation.

THE FATHER AS CREATOR

There is practically no dispute among professing Christians that God the Father is the Creator. To speak of the Father is to speak of God, and the Bible consistently reveals God as the Creator of all. As the prophet Isaiah writes, "God is enthroned above the circle of the earth ... He stretches out the heavens like thin cloth and spreads them out like a tent to live in.... 'To whom will you compare me, or who is my equal?' asks the Holy One. Look up and see! Who created these? He brings out the stars by number; he calls all of them by name. Because of his great power and strength, not one of them is missing.... Do you not know? Have you not heard? The Lord is the everlasting God, the Creator of the whole earth" (Isa. 40:22, 25-26, 28).

Other Old Testament verses tell us of God's creative work, for example:

Nehemiah 9:6 – "You, Lord, are the only God. You created the heavens, the highest heavens with all their stars, the earth and all that is on it, the seas and all that is in them. You give life to all of them, and all the stars of heaven worship you."

Job 9:8-9 – "He alone stretches out the heavens and treads on the waves of the sea. He makes the stars: the Bear, Orion, the Pleiades, and the constellations of the southern sky."

Psalm 33:6 – "The heavens were made by the word of the Lord, and all the stars, by the breath of his mouth." It's interesting to note the psalmist's mention of the "word" of the Lord and the "breath" of His mouth. Elsewhere in Scripture, we see Jesus depicted as the eternally existing "Word" (John 1:1), while the Hebrew word for "breath" often describes the Holy Spirit. There is a hint of the Trinity's united work of creation in this single verse.

Psalm 121:2 – "My help comes from the Lord, the Maker of heaven and earth."

Isaiah 42:5 – "This is what God, the Lord, says – who created the heavens and stretched them out, who spread out the earth and what comes from it, who gives breath to the people on it and spirit to those who walk on it ..."

Isaiah 44:24 – "I am the Lord, who made everything; who stretched out the heavens by myself; who alone spread out the earth."

Isaiah 45:18 – "For this is what the Lord says – the

Creator of the heavens, the God who formed the earth and made it, the one who established it ..."

The New Testament picks up this theme in passages such as:

Ephesians 3:9 – Grace is given to the apostle Paul to "shed light for all about the administration of the mystery hidden for ages in God who created all things."

Hebrews 11:3 – "By faith we understand that the universe was created by the word of God, so that what is seen was made from things that are not visible."

Revelation 4:11 – The twenty-four elders fall down before the one seated on the throne in heaven, casting their crowns before the throne and declaring, "Our Lord and God, you are worthy to receive glory and honor and power, because you have created all things, and by your will they exist and were created."

One other key New Testament passage comes from the pen of the apostle Paul, who writes, "yet for us there is one God, the Father. All things are from him, and we exist for him" (1 Cor. 8:6). This is a clear reference to the creative work of the Father. But Paul doesn't stop there: "And there is one Lord, Jesus Christ. All things are through him, and we exist through him" (v. 6).

So, while both the Old and New Testaments depict the Father as the Creator of all things, Paul gives the Corinthians – and us – a glimpse into the reality that Jesus engaged fully in the Father's creative acts. We are about to see this in more detail.

THE SON AS CREATOR

In Chapters Six and Seven, we explored the Incarnation, in which the eternal Son of God adds sinless humanity to His deity through the miracle of the virgin birth, thus becoming the God-Man. If in fact Jesus exists eternally and is uncreated, then He rightly may be seen as the Creator of all, since, as James White notes, "He who *creates* cannot himself be *created*. Hence, the eternality of Christ is directly related to His being the Maker of all things."[1]

Let's consider several passages that reveal the Son as Creator.

John 1:3 – "All things were created through him, and apart from him not one thing was created that has been created."

After establishing that Jesus is both eternal and divine, as well as a distinct person from the Father (vv. 1-2), John declares that the Son created "all things." This simple statement sets Christianity apart from Gnosticism, a religious movement that severely threatened the infant church, particularly in the second and third centuries.

While diverse, Gnosticism generally held to two overarching beliefs. First, salvation is obtained primarily through special knowledge obtained in secret rituals. In fact, the term *gnosticism* comes from the Greek word *gnosis*, meaning "knowledge." This secretly obtained knowledge enables a person to escape the corruption of the world, particularly as it resides in the physical body.

Second, Gnostics embraced dualism. That is, they believed the material world is inherently evil, while the spiritual realm is intrinsically good. So, salvation is achieved by escaping the body – freeing the "good" spirit from the "evil" flesh. This may be one reason the Greeks on Mars Hill berated Paul for preaching the resurrection of the body (Acts 17:32). After all, if the body is evil, who wants a resurrected one?

In any case, Gnostics faced the challenge of explaining who created the world. If God is pure spirit, and if matter is corrupt, how can the two be reconciled? Gnostics devised their own creation story. It begins with God – a good, pure, and holy spirit. From God flows a series of "emanations" known as *aeons*. These are godlike creatures sometimes associated with the angels of Judaism and Christianity. Together, all of the *aeons* make up the *pleroma*, the Greek word for "fullness." Each *aeon* is a little less pure than the previous one, but finally we get to the *Demiurge*, a divine being with the capacity to create and come into contact with the material world. Some second-century Gnostic leaders identified the *Demiurge* with Yahweh.[2]

It's difficult to know the extent of Gnostic influence in John's mind as he pens his Gospel. However, in 1 John 4, he addresses another Gnostic heresy known as *Docetism*, which denied that Jesus had a physical body. Docetics accepted Christ's deity but not His humanity, saying He only "seemed" to walk this world in the flesh. They took their name from the Greek term *dokein*, which means "to seem."

This is why John writes, "This is how you know the Spirit of God: Every spirit [person who claims divine gifting for service] that confesses that Jesus Christ has come in the flesh is from God, but every spirit that does not confess Jesus is not from God. This is the spirit of the antichrist, which you have heard is coming; even now already it is in the world" (1 John 4:2-3). In other words, to deny the Incarnation is to expose the spirit of the antichrist.

With all of this as a backdrop, we can see John 1:1-3 as a doctrinal North Star to guide the early church. Jesus is eternal. He is uncreated. He is distinct from God the Father but with Him, face-to-face, in the beginning. He *is* God. And He created *all* things. Not all other things, excluding Himself. If Jesus is a created being – as Gnostics believed centuries ago and Jehovah's Witnesses teach today – then He is a "thing" who must Himself be created. But no, the apostle John makes clear: Jesus created "all things."

Colossians 1:15-17 – "He [Jesus] is the image of the invisible God, the firstborn over all creation. For everything was created by him, in heaven and on earth, the visible and the invisible, whether thrones or dominions or rulers or authorities – all things have been created through him and for him. He is before all things, and by him all things hold together."

Those who seek to reduce Jesus to a created being argue that Paul refers to Jesus as the *image* of the invisible God, not God Himself. But this fails to recognize that Jesus and the Father are distinct divine persons. Further, no mere creature can serve as the true image of the invisible God. Humans are created to be *image bearers* of God, reflecting His character and attributes, but we are not divine. Only Jesus, who shares the eternal glory of the Father, can truly reveal Him in human flesh (John 17:5).

Then, some contend that Jesus, as the "firstborn over all creation," is the first of God's created beings. Jehovah's Witnesses are the primary promoters of this view today. Others, like Latter-day Saints, argue that "firstborn" implies a relationship between the Father and Son in which the Son is inferior, at least temporarily.

But the Greek *prototokos* (firstborn), while it can refer to the first person born into a family, often signifies a position of supremacy. For example, Jesus is the "firstborn among many brothers and sisters," the model of all saints bound for glory (Rom. 8:29). In Hebrews 1:6, the Father "brings his firstborn into the world," with the result being that "all God's angels worship him." In Colossians 1:18 and Revelation 1:5, Jesus is the "firstborn from the dead," the first to be raised in a glorified body, which serves as the prototype for our future resurrected bodies.

So, as Paul describes Jesus as "the firstborn over all creation," he has two thoughts in mind, according to Greek scholar Kenneth Wuest: "priority to all creation and sovereignty over all creation. In the first meaning we see the absolute preexistence of the Logos. Since our Lord existed before all created things, He must be uncreated. Since He is uncreated, He is eternal. Since He is eternal, He is God. Since He is

God, He cannot be one of the emanations from deity of which the Gnostic speaks.... In the second meaning we see that He is the natural ruler, the acknowledged head of God's household."[3]

This brings us to a clear understanding of Paul's message. As the divine second person of the Trinity, the uncreated Creator, Jesus is sovereign over *all* creation. That's because He created *everything* – not just the natural world in which we live, but the unseen realm of angelic beings. All things are created through Him and for Him, and He holds them all together. Jesus is not a mere secondary deity or an exalted man; He is the Creator of and sovereign ruler over the realms of spirit and matter.

Hebrews 1:1-3 – "Long ago God spoke to the fathers by the prophets at different times and in different ways. In these last days, he has spoken to us by his Son. God has appointed him heir of all things and made the universe through him. The Son is the radiance of God's glory and the exact expression of his nature, sustaining all things by his powerful word. After making purification for sins, he sat down at the right hand of the Majesty on high."

The author of Hebrews makes much of Jesus' superiority to angels and human beings. That's because Jesus is divine, eternal, and the Creator of all. As the "exact expression" of God's nature, He bears the divine imprint in His human flesh. As Marvin Vincent comments, "Here the essential being of God is conceived as setting its distinctive stamp upon Christ, coming into definite and characteristic expression in his person, so that the Son bears the exact impress of the divine nature and character."[4]

Some may argue that because the writer of Hebrews says God made the universe *through* Jesus, Jesus is a secondary creator, or a mere tool that the Father employed to create all things. But this fails to take into account the writer's emphasis on the deity of Christ in verse 3: the "radiance of God's glory and the exact expression of his nature." Christ is not a passive instrument in creation. Rather, He is a cooperating agent.

Further, Jesus is depicted as "sustaining all things by his powerful word." This is more than holding the dead weight of the world on His shoulders, or serving as a helmsman to pilot the universe through its natural course. No, the Creator of all is in control of all. He sovereignly maintains it and ensures that it fulfills the purpose for which everything was made. He even steps into human history to make "purification for sins," and then assumes His rightful place at the right hand of the Majesty on high (v. 3).

Revelation 5:11-14 – "Then I looked and heard the voice of many angels around the throne, and also of the living creatures and of the elders. Their number was countless thousands, plus thousands of thousands. They said with a loud voice, Worthy is the Lamb who was slaughtered to receive power and riches and wisdom and strength and honor and glory and blessing! I heard every creature in heaven, on earth, under the earth, on the sea, and everything in them say, Blessing and honor and glory and power be to the one seated on the throne, and to the Lamb, forever and ever!"

This passage might slip our notice with respect to Jesus as the Creator. So, we should take note of who worships the Lamb: "*every creature* in heaven, on earth, under the earth, on the sea, and everything in them" (emphasis added). Clearly, as God, Jesus receives worship, and as Creator, He is honored by *all* creatures.

THE HOLY SPIRIT AS CREATOR

If the Bible reveals the Father and Son as co-creators of everything, what role does the Holy Spirit play? Is He an instrument of creation – an impersonal force like the noonday sun hardening clay, or wind stirring up waves on the water? To the contrary, from the first chapter of Genesis onward, we see the Spirit as a personal, almighty person who puts His shoulder into the work of creation along with the Father and the Son.

Genesis 1:2 declares, "Now the earth was formless and empty, darkness covered the surface of the watery depths, and the Spirit of God was hovering over the surface of the waters." The word translated "hovering" means brooding, as a bird hatching her eggs. It is the same word used in Deuteronomy 32:11, where Moses declares that Yahweh "watches over his nest like an eagle and *hovers* over his young; he spreads his wings, catches him, and carries him on his feathers" (emphasis added).

As one commentary puts it, "The immediate agency of the Spirit, by working on the dead and discordant elements, combined, arranged, and ripened them into a state adapted for being the scene of a new creation."[5] Andrew Knowles adds, "There is nothing remote or detached about the way God works. He is a 'hands-on' creator, keenly committed to this marvelous work, absorbed in concentration and fizzing with enthusiasm. His Spirit moves to shape the chaos, fill the void, lighten the darkness and bring a universe to life."[6]

Job offers a unique insight into the work of the Holy Spirit in Job 33:4: "The Spirit of God has made me, and the breath of the Almighty gives me life." There is striking parallelism in this verse. The Holy Spirit is identified by two different words: *ruwach* (wind, breath, exhalation) and *neshamaw* (wind, vital breath, divine inspiration, intellect). God is given two different names: *el* (God) and *Shadday* (Almighty). And there are two different verbs used to designate the act of creation: *asah* (made) and *chayah* (keep alive; give life).

Robert Morey notes, "The verb 'made me' refers to an act of divine creation. It is the word used for the creative acts of God in Genesis 1:31; 2:2; 3:1; 5:1, etc. It is even translated 'Maker' in Job 32:22. Job's choice of this particular Hebrew word is significant because it clearly reveals that he understood in some sense the Spirit of God is God."⁷

In speaking about God the Creator, Job tells his companion Bildad, "His Spirit made the heavens beautiful" (Job 26:13 NLT). The psalmist declares, "The heavens were made by the word of the Lord, and all the stars, by the breath [spirit] of his mouth" (Ps. 33:6).

In a psalm extolling the creative works of God, the psalmist writes, "When you send your Spirit, they [God's creatures] are created, and you renew the face of the ground" (Ps. 104:30 NIV).

We should note that the Bible describes another "hovering" of the Holy Spirit similar to His work of creation in Genesis 1:2. It is a stunning miracle, never to be repeated – the conception of Jesus in the womb of the virgin Mary. Luke describes it this way: "The angel [Gabriel] replied to her [Mary]: 'The Holy Spirit will come upon you, and the power of the Most High will overshadow you. Therefore, the holy one to be born will be called the Son of God'" (Luke 1:35).

As the Holy Spirit is the agent of the Incarnation, He also brings new life to sinners as they repent and receive the Lord Jesus Christ. Jesus tells Nicodemus, "Truly I tell you, unless someone is born of water and the Spirit, he cannot enter the kingdom of God" (John 3:5). Later, after feeding the five thousand and declaring Himself the bread of life, Jesus watches many disciples desert Him because they cannot accept His call to complete devotion. He tells His followers, "The Spirit is the one who gives life. The flesh doesn't help at all. The words that I have spoken to you are spirit and are life" (John 6:63).

Later, the apostle Paul writes, "[H]e saved us – not by works of righteousness that we had done, but according to his mercy – through the washing of regeneration and renewal by the Holy Spirit" (Titus 3:5). It is clear that the Holy Spirit shares in the creative and redemptive work of the Father and the Son.

PERICHORESIS

One final thought about creation may help us see the collaborative work of the Trinity as an extension of the interdependent nature of the Father, Son, and Holy Spirit. *Perichoresis* is an ancient theme enjoying a modern-day revival. As Millard Erickson explains, "This is the idea of the interpenetration of life and personality within the Godhead, the idea that the Father, Son, and Holy Spirit are bound together in such a close unity that the life of each flows through each of the others, and each has access to the thought and experience of others."[8] This means, of course, that God from all eternity is both spirit and personal, although Jesus takes on human flesh in the Incarnation. The material universe came into existence through the creative act of the triune God.

Further, the concept of *perichoresis* means not only that the three members of the Godhead share their lives with one another, but that all three are involved in *all* the works of God. Some of these works are primarily the doing of one person, but all three participate in some sense. Jesus, for example, becomes incarnate, suffers and dies on the cross for our sins, and rises from the dead to conquer Satan, sin, and death. Yet, the Father and the Spirit play unique supporting roles, as we see in the next chapter.

As for creation, the Bible progressively reveals the manner in which all three members of the Godhead work together. Old Testament writers generally attribute creation to God, while New Testament authors offer a wider perspective. One example is Paul's statement in 1 Corinthians 8:6: "[Y]et for us there is one God, the Father. All things are from him, and we exist for him. And there is one Lord, Jesus Christ. All things are through him, and we exist through him." The apostle indicates that creation depends on both the Father and the Son.

John 1:3, Colossians 1:16, Hebrews 1:10, and other New Testament passages contribute to the idea that Jesus created all things. Meanwhile, Old Testament passages like Genesis 1:2, Job 26:13, Psalm 104:30, and Isaiah 40:12-13 indicate the participation of the Holy Spirit in creation.

Erickson uses the analogy of construction to illustrate how the Father, Son, and Holy Spirit all may be said to create. When asked, "Who built that house?" we might be thinking of the architect, the general contractor, the supplier of materials, the bank, or even the owners who end up paying for the entire structure over time. So, writes Erickson, "it is possible to think of the Father as the originator or source of the creation, the Son as the designer or organizer of the creation, and the Spirit as the executor of the act of creation, the one who actually carries it out."[9]

SUMMARY

The persons of the Godhead are three distinguishable centers of consciousness within one being. They interact with one another. Their lives flow through the others. None could exist independently of the others. Each experiences the consciousness of the others.

As a result, while either the Father, Son, or Holy Spirit is revealed as the primary agent in certain works – such as creation or redemption – none of them acts alone. This may not resolve every issue relating to the doctrine of the Trinity, but it should help us see the way in which the distinct persons of the Godhead are unified in essence and work.

REVIEW

1. Although Scripture most clearly depicts God the _____ as Creator, we may see that He never acts independently. Rather, He works in concert with the _____

and the Holy Spirit. This includes the Godhead's
_____ work of creation.

2. Look up the following Scriptures and identify which persons of the Godhead are engaged in creation. Note that some passages involve more than one member of the Trinity.

(a) Genesis 1:2

_____

(b) Job 9:8-9

_____

(c) John 1:3

_____

(d) 1 Corinthians 8:6

_____

(e) Hebrews 1:1-3

_____

(f) Revelation 4:11

_____

3. John 1:1-3 served as a doctrinal North Star to guide the early church, which wrestled with a heresy known as _____. Among other false beliefs, this religious movement embraced _____, the belief that

the material world is evil, while the spiritual realm is good. Thus, for Jesus to be human, He must be created and less than completely pure. But John tells us the Word is _____ ("In the beginning") and uncreated. What's more, He is the Creator of _____ things.

4. The Holy Spirit is not an impersonal _____ that God used to create the material world. To the contrary, from the first chapter of Genesis onward, we see the Spirit as a _____, almighty being who puts His shoulder into the work of creation along with the Father and the Son.

5. The ancient concept of *perichoresis* means not only that the three members of the Godhead share their _____ with one another, but that all three are involved in *all* of the _____ of God. Some of these works are primarily the doing of one person, but all three participate in some sense. Jesus, for example, becomes incarnate, suffers and _____ on the cross for our sins, and rises from the dead. Yet, the Father and the Spirit play unique _____ roles in our redemption.

THINK

Questions for personal or group study

1. Why do you think the authors of Scripture never try to prove the existence of God? For those who struggle with believing in God, how does the Bible point to evidence in the natural world of a divine Designer and a divine moral Law Giver? Consider Romans 1:18-32; 2:12-16.

2. The apostle Paul writes that Jesus is "the image of the invis-

ible God, the firstborn over all creation" (Col. 1:15). Jehovah's Witnesses cite this verse to argue that Jehovah first created Jesus, who then created all other things. Why is this a wrong understanding of Paul's teaching?

3. When Moses writes that the Spirit of God was "hovering" or "moving" over the surface of the waters (Gen. 1:2), how does that depict the willful actions of a person rather than the guided movements of an impersonal force? How do Deuteronomy 32:11, Job 33:14, and Psalm 104:30 help show the personal, creative work of the Spirit? What other creative work does the Spirit do in John 3:5, 6:63, and Titus 3:5?

4. We briefly addressed the ancient theme of *perichoresis*, which teaches that the Father, Son, and Holy Spirit are bound together in such close unity that the life of each flows through each of the others, and each has access to the thoughts and experiences of the others. What impact does that have on the creation of all things?

5. Why did it take three persons – Father, Son, and Holy Spirit – to create everything? If all members of the Godhead are co-equal and co-eternal, all-powerful and all-knowing, why couldn't just the Father, Son, or Holy Spirit bring everything into existence?

CHAPTER TEN

The Trinity and Salvation

The Bible clearly teaches that Jesus is our Savior. He is the promised "seed" of woman who crushes the head of Satan (Gen. 3:15). He is the Suffering Servant who bears our griefs and carries our sorrows (Isa. 52:13 – 53:12). He is the Lamb of God who takes away the sin of the world (John 1:29). He comes to seek and to save the lost (Luke 19:10). He is the way, the truth, and the life (John 14:6); the bread of life (John 6:51); the door (John 10:9); the good shepherd who lays down His life for the sheep (John 10:11); the resurrection and the life (John 11:25); and much more. He came into this world to die – to give His life as a ransom for many (Matt. 20:28). Jesus is, indeed, our great God and Savior (Titus 2:13).

A cursory reading of Scripture reveals God's plan to redeem sinful and fallen people through the sacrificial and substitutionary death of Jesus of Nazareth. He truly is our Savior, and salvation is found in no one else (Acts 4:11-12). And yet, as in the Trinity's work of creation, no single member of the Godhead acts alone. As we explore briefly in this chapter, the Father, Son, and Holy Spirit all play important, complementary roles in saving us from sin and restoring us to a right relationship with God.

Various Christian sects and cults embrace Jesus as Savior while denying the doctrine of the Trinity. But can Jesus really be our Savior if He is a created being? Or if He is one god in an unbroken line of many others like Him? Or if He is only the present manifestation of God, indistinguishable from the Father and the Holy Spirit? We cannot grasp a proper understanding of salvation apart from the Trinity. More to the point, we cannot be saved apart from the Trinity.

Historically, Christians have believed that salvation – God's remedy for sin and its consequences – is secured only because the second person of the Trinity added sinless humanity to His deity through the miracle of the virgin birth. The God-Man bore our sins on the cross and rose from the dead to conquer Satan, sin, and death on our behalf. As divine, Jesus possessed the eternal nature necessary to pay the eternal debt humanity owes its offended Creator. As a man, He experienced the full range of what it means to be human, including every form of temptation. Yet, He remained sinless (Heb. 4:15).

After finishing the work for which He was sent, Jesus presented Himself to the Father as the perfect sacrifice for our sins, becoming the "source of eternal salvation" (Heb. 5:9). On that basis, the Father forgave our sins, and the Holy Spirit conferred new life to believing sinners. As Millard Erickson states, "If the doctrine of the Trinity is not true, then the understanding of salvation must be modified."[1]

TRINITARIAN PRAISE

Since the Father, Son, and Holy Spirit constitute one divine being – one God – the work of salvation is shared among the members of the Trinity. No single member delivers all the elements of salvation, but together they accomplish all the work that produces redemption.

Ephesians 1:3-14 is a good illustration of a Trinitarian

expression of praise. In verses 3-6, Paul praises the Father for choosing us. In verses 7-12, he exalts Jesus for dying for us. And in verses 13-14, he honors the Spirit for sealing us. Let's look more closely:

Ephesians 1:3-6 – "Blessed is the God and Father of our Lord Jesus Christ, who has blessed us with every spiritual blessing in the heavens in Christ. For he chose us in him, before the foundation of the world, to be holy and blameless in love before him. He predestined us to be adopted as sons through Jesus Christ for himself, according to the good pleasure of his will, to the praise of his glorious grace that he lavished on us in the Beloved One."

Whatever your views on the doctrine of divine election,[2] it's indisputable that the Father plays a vital role in our salvation. Specifically, He grants us every spiritual blessing in the heavenly realm. He chooses us in Christ in eternity past, so that we are reckoned as blameless before Him, just as Jesus is blameless. And He predestines us to be His adopted children through the finished work of Christ. Much more could be said about these weighty verses, but it is clear that the work of the Father and the Son in our salvation may be distinguished but not separated. The Father blesses, chooses, and adopts us as His own.

From these verses, we may draw the twin truths that the Father is the one who elects, and the Son is the one through whom election is realized. Jesus – the way, the truth, and the life – ensures that all those given to Him are never lost.

Ephesians 1:7-12 – "In him we have redemption through his blood, the forgiveness of our trespasses, according to the riches of his grace that he richly poured out on us with all wisdom and understanding. He made known to us the mystery of his will, according to his good pleasure that he purposed in Christ as a plan for the right time – to bring everything together in Christ, both things in heaven and things on earth in him. In him we have also received an inheritance, because we were predestined according to the plan of the one who works out everything in agreement with the purpose of his will, so that we who had already put our hope in Christ might bring praise to his glory."

The blood of Jesus, shed on Calvary, purchased the forgiveness of our sins, made us children of the Father through the new birth, and secured our inheritance as coheirs of all things with Jesus. Paul does not depict Jesus as the one who chooses, predestines, or adopts us, but He is the one who completes the work necessary for all of these blessings to be received as our sin debt is cancelled and we are restored to a right relationship with God.

Ephesians 1:13-14 – "In him you also – when you heard the word of truth, the gospel of your salvation, and when you also believed – were sealed in him with the promised Holy Spirit. He is the down payment of our inheritance, until the redemption of the possession, to the praise of his glory."

Being forgiven of our sins, granted a new birth, and adopted into God's family, we are sealed by the Holy Spirit, who places God's mark of ownership on us; Satan no longer may lay claim to us. What's more, we are joint heirs with Jesus of all things. To secure that promise, the Holy Spirit serves as the guarantee – the "earnest money," if you will – of our place in God's everlasting kingdom.

A few chapters later, Paul cautions the Ephesian believers not to "grieve God's Holy Spirit. You were sealed by him for the day of redemption" (Eph. 4:30). And in 2 Corinthians 1:22, the apostle writes, "He [God] has also put his seal on us and given us the Spirit in our hearts as a down payment."

Together, these verses show that the triune Godhead works in complete unity to secure the salvation of believing sinners. The Father, Son, and Holy Spirit carry out distinct roles, but they do so with a singular purpose so that the Father's election cannot be separated from the Son's sacrifice, which cannot be separated from the Spirit's sealing. This necessitates the deity of all three members of the Godhead, the distinctiveness of their persons, the uniqueness of their roles in salvation, and the unity of their love and purpose.

Is it any wonder that non-Trinitarian Christian sects and cults fail to adequately capture the wonder of salvation by grace alone, through faith alone, in Christ alone?

FACETS OF SALVATION

Stated simply, salvation is God's remedy for the sin that has ruined everything and alienated everyone from Him. The Lord reveals this remedy as soon as Adam and Eve rebel against Him. He promises a future Redeemer who crushes the head of Satan (Gen. 3:15). Then, He provides additional promises throughout the Old Testament, granting us more than four hundred prophecies, appearances, or foreshadowings of the Messiah, a King who comes as a virgin-born child in Bethlehem.[3]

This child, Jesus of Nazareth, bursts onto the scene at just the right time (Gal. 4:4). He lives a sinless life and dies on a Roman cross, taking upon Himself our sins and paying the penalty of death for them (2 Cor. 5:21). Then, He rises physically from the dead on the third day, conquering Satan, sin, and death, and freely offering forgiveness of sins and everlasting life by grace through faith in Him. Before ascending into heaven, He promises to return one day to fulfill all things – that is, to complete His work of salvation and to set everything right (Matt. 16:27; 25:31-46; John 14:1-3).

For followers of Jesus, salvation is experienced as an everlasting, unbreakable relationship with Him. It has both temporal and eternal benefits. Consider, for example, that we are *foreknown*, *elected*, and *predestined* in eternity past. Put another way, we are saved before time began.

Other elements of salvation are experienced personally

within our lifetimes as God *calls* us to Himself; *regenerates* us, or makes us spiritually alive; *justifies* us, or declares us in right standing before Him; *indwells* us, or takes up permanent residence in our human spirits; *baptizes* us in the Holy Spirit, or places us positionally into the church; *sanctifies* us, or sets us apart and begins the process of making us more like Christ; *adopts* us into His family; and *seals* us, or places His mark of ownership on us.

One day, the final act of salvation is completed in *glorification*. We are physically resurrected and given incorruptible bodies similar to the resurrected body of our Savior.

We have just mentioned twelve Bible terms that describe God's work of redemption. While there are other terms – redemption, conversion, propitiation, and reconciliation, to name a few – these twelve terms illustrate as simply as possible God's glorious plan of salvation, woven as a divine tapestry, spanning time and eternity. These are not twelve separate works that God cobbles together. Rather, they are elements of a unified whole.

Put another way, we may imagine God's work of salvation as a perfectly sculpted diamond, with its many facets illuminating, in unique ways, the glorious beauty of God's redemptive work. While no mere image does justice to the splendor of salvation, perhaps the thought of a diamond helps us see that salvation is one, singular, multi-faceted work of God that stretches from eternity past to eternity future. As such, those who by faith are "in Christ" may be assured that He completes the good work He started in us long ago (Phil. 1:6).

Let's take a moment to explore these twelve facets of salvation.

Salvation Before Time

Foreknowledge means more than knowing facts beforehand; it means our omniscient God always has known believers and has reckoned us predestined, called, justified, and glorified (Rom. 8:29-30). This encompasses the unsearchable depths of God's sovereignty and the certainty of a human response in faith to the gospel message.

Election is God's choice of certain individuals to salvation before the foundation of the world. The Reformed (Calvinist) position on election is that it is *unconditional*; that is, God selected specific persons for everlasting life based solely on His divine will and good pleasure, not on foreseen faith. The non-Reformed (Arminian) view is that election is *conditional*; in other words, God selected specific persons for salvation based on foreseeing that they would respond in belief and repentance to the gospel message.

Predestination is God's plan from eternity past to complete the work of redemption in every saint, fully conforming us to the image of His Son. Predestination cannot be separated from His other works of redemption before time, in time, or beyond time. From a human standpoint, God's predestination from the farthest reaches of eternity invades time, applies to us, and continues out into eternity future in glorification.

These three facets of salvation *before time* – foreknowledge, election, and predestination – cannot be divorced from human responsibility. God's sovereignty, and the endowed right of people to make decisions for which we are held accountable, are parallel biblical truths. Where they intersect in the mind of God is a wondrous mystery to His creatures.

Salvation in Time

Calling involves both a general call as the gospel is proclaimed, and an effectual call in which those whom God foreknew, elected, and predestined are drawn to Christ, resulting in belief and repentance. God's sovereignty and human responsibility are mysteriously bound together in calling.

Regeneration is the work of the Holy Spirit that brings a sinner from spiritual death to spiritual life; it often is referred to as being "born again" or "born from above."

Justification is a legal declaration in heaven. There, Christ's perfect righteousness is transferred to the account of believing sinners, while our sin debt is transferred to His account, so that we are acquitted before the Father's holy bench.

Indwelling is a divine act in which the Holy Spirit takes up permanent residence in the body of a believer in Jesus Christ. Followers of Jesus are indwelt once, and permanently.

Baptism in the Holy Spirit is the means by which God places new believers into the body of Christ. Thus, all Christians – whom the Holy Spirit has regenerated and indwelt – share the common bond of the Spirit as members of the universal, or invisible, church.

Sanctification is the work of God making followers of Jesus more like our Savior. It may be understood in two ways, both of which relate to holiness. First, there is *positional* sanctification, the state of being set apart for God. Second, there is *practical* sanctification, the lifelong process by which the Holy Spirit makes us more like Jesus.

Adoption is the Father's gracious act of making new Christians members of His family. Having been born again, we are adopted by the Father as His sons and daughters. And, incredibly, this makes us coheirs with Jesus, the eternal Son of God – a sharing of spiritual wealth and privilege that prompts Jesus to burst with joy, not jealousy.

Sealing is part of the gift of the Holy Spirit granted to new believers as God places His divine mark of ownership on us, thus ensuring His everlasting presence and our eternal security.

Many of these facets of salvation are applied instantaneously as one-time, non-repeatable acts of God, with benefits extending throughout our lifetimes and into eternity future. Sanctification is different in that it is both a singular act and an ongoing process that meets its apex in glorification. In any case, all eight of these works of redemption *in time* are permanent and irrevocable.

Salvation Beyond Time

Glorification is the final stage in God's work of salvation. It is the crowning achievement of sanctification, in which Christians are fully conformed to the image of Christ. It is the perfection of the body, as well as the soul and spirit. Even more, it is the restoration of all creation to its pristine innocence.

Put another way, glorification is the means by which God fully reverses the effects of the Fall, purging sin and its stain from our lives and from the created order. It involves the return of Jesus, the future resurrection and judgment of all people, and the creation of new heavens and a new earth.

Taken together, these twelve facets of salvation reveal the wondrous scope of God's plan to call out a people for Himself. It is biblically faithful for followers of Jesus to say we *were* saved (from the penalty of sin); we *are being* saved (from the power of sin); and we *will be* saved (from the presence of sin).

So, what does the Trinity have to do with all of this?

THE TRINITY IN SALVATION

In Chapter Four, we noted that there are seventy-five Trinitarian references in the New Testament.[4] Many of these passages reveal the collaborative work of the Father, Son, and Holy Spirit in securing our salvation. Space does not permit a full exploration of every reference, but we list several for the purpose of demonstrating how the Trinity is woven into the fabric of the greatest story ever told.

Note the italicized terms in the commentary beneath each

Scripture passage, and refer back to the "Facets of Salvation" section for definitions and more details.

Romans 5:1-6 – "Therefore, since we have been declared righteous by faith, we have peace with God through our Lord Jesus Christ. We have also obtained access through him by faith into this grace in which we stand, and we rejoice in the hope of the glory of God.... This hope will not disappoint us, because God's love has been poured out in our hearts through the Holy Spirit who was given to us."

Through the finished work of Christ, we obtain *justification*, the Father's declaration of our righteousness, and thus we are no longer His enemies. In addition, we rejoice in the confident expectation (hope) that God finishes the good work He started in us (see Phil. 1:6), reaching its climax in *glorification*, where we are fully conformed to the image of Christ. *Sealing* these promises is the Holy Spirit, who *indwells* us.

Romans 8:14-17 – "For all those led by God's Spirit are God's sons. You did not receive a spirit of slavery to fall back into fear. Instead, you received the Spirit of adoption, by whom we cry out, '*Abba*, Father!' The Spirit himself testifies together with our spirit that we are God's children, and if children, also heirs – heirs of God and coheirs with Christ – if indeed we suffer with him so that we may also be glorified with him."

Followers of Jesus have received the *indwelling* Holy Spirit, who also serves as the agent in our *adoption* as sons and daughters of the Father. As adopted children, we are coheirs with Jesus in His inheritance of all things. This includes *glorification*, which is received when we are resurrected from the dead and clothed in Christ's immortality. Paul shares a similar message of the Trinity's work of adoption in Galatians 4:4-7.

1 Corinthians 6:9-11 – "Don't you know that the unrighteous will not inherit God's kingdom? Do not be deceived: No sexually immoral people, idolaters, adulterers, or males who have sex with males, no thieves, greedy people, drunkards, verbally abusive people, or swindlers will inherit God's kingdom. And some of you used to be like this. But you were washed, you were sanctified, you were justified in the name of the Lord Jesus Christ and by the Spirit of our God."

Entrance into God's kingdom requires a transformation of character that only comes through the finished work of Jesus on the cross and the power of the Holy Spirit. Believing sinners are *regenerated*, or born again (washed), *sanctified*, or set apart as God's own, and *justified*, or declared in right standing with the Father.

2 Corinthians 1:21-22 – "Now it is God who strengthens us together with you in Christ, and who has anointed us. He has also put his seal on us and given us the Spirit in our hearts as a down payment."

God the Father anoints believers in Jesus with the Holy Spirit. That is, the Spirit *regenerates* us, or makes us spiritually alive. He also *indwells* us, places us positionally into the body of Christ in *Spirit baptism*, sets us apart in *sanctification*, and *seals* us, or places God's mark of ownership on us, freeing us from the slave market of sin.

Ephesians 2:18 - "For through him [Jesus] we both [Jews and Gentiles] have access in one Spirit to the Father" (ESV).

Here we see the three persons of the Trinity listed together as bringing about our salvation. Christ has reconciled Jews and Gentiles to God in one body through the cross (v. 16). The Spirit *calls* us to Christ, then *regenerates*, *indwells*, *seals*, and *sanctifies* us. The Spirit also ensures our *adoption* as children of the Father.

While the Father, Son, and Holy Spirit engage in saving works unique to their functions within the Godhead, they do not act alone. Rather, they work together. "To draw near to God and to enjoy him forever in a new creation is both mankind's greatest good and the ultimate accomplishment of Christ's earthly work of redemption."[5]

2 Thessalonians 2:13-14 – "But we ought to thank God always for you, brothers and sisters loved by the Lord, because from the beginning God has chosen you for salvation through sanctification by the Spirit and through belief in the truth. He called you to this through our gospel, so that you might obtain the glory of our Lord Jesus Christ."

From the beginning – that is, before the creation of the world – the Father *chose / elected* followers of Jesus. This action was grounded in His *foreknowledge* (see Rom. 8:29-30). The means God uses to bring about salvation, in addition to the finished work of Christ, is the work of the Holy Spirit, who *calls, regenerates, indwells, baptizes in the Spirit, seals,* and *sanctifies*. The human aspect of salvation is "belief in the truth" of the gospel.

Titus 3:4-7 – "But when the kindness of God our Savior and his love for mankind appeared, he saved us – not by works of righteousness that we had done but according to his mercy – through the washing of regeneration and renewal by the Holy Spirit. He poured out his Spirit on us abundantly through Jesus Christ our Savior so that, having been justified by his grace, we may become heirs with the hope of eternal life."

Note first of all that both the Father and Jesus are depicted as "Savior." Titus 1:3 refers to "God our Savior," and the Greek in Titus 3:4 reads, "our Savior God," a reference to the Father.[6] But Paul also refers to Jesus Christ as our Savior. The emphasis in this passage is not on man's response in faith so much as it is on God's initiative in salvation.

God saves us through the washing of *regeneration* and renewal by the Holy Spirit – the new birth. When Jesus completes His work of redemption, He sends the Holy Spirit, who convicts the unbelieving world and *indwells* believers (see John 14:16-17, 26; 15:26; 16:7-15). Paul further assures us that we are *justified* by grace, a work of the Father. Finally, we are *adopted* children of the Father, coheirs with Jesus, and we share the confident expectation of eternal life, which reaches its zenith in *glorification*.

Hebrews 10:29-30 – "How much worse punishment do you think one will deserve who has trampled on the Son of God, who has regarded as profane the blood of the covenant by which he was sanctified, and who has insulted the Spirit of grace? For we know the one who has said, Vengeance belongs to me; I will repay, and again, The Lord will judge his people."

In a stern warning against deliberate sin, the writer of Hebrews reminds us that the blood of Jesus *sanctifies* us, or sets us apart. As he notes in verse 10 of the same chapter, "we have been sanctified through the offering of the body of Jesus Christ once for all time." While sanctification is a work normally ascribed to the Holy Spirit, we see here how the persons of the Godhead work together for our salvation.

In addition, the writer notes that the one who treats the blood of Jesus as common, or profane, insults the Spirit. Finally, the writer warns that the Father ("the Lord") executes judgment, although we see in other passages that Jesus is the Judge (John 5:22) and the Holy Spirit sometimes plays a role in judgment (Acts 5:1-11).

1 Peter 1:1-2 – "Peter, an apostle of Jesus Christ: To those chosen, living as exiles dispersed abroad in Pontus, Galatia, Cappadocia, Asia, and Bithynia, chosen according to the foreknowledge of God the Father, through the sanctifying work of the Spirit, to be obedient and to be sprinkled with the blood of Jesus Christ ..."

Peter describes Christians as chosen, or *elected*, according to the *foreknowledge* of God the Father. We also are *sanctified*, or set apart and made holy, by the Holy Spirit. All of this hinges on the blood of Jesus, who cleanses us from sin. In a passage known as the "golden chain of redemption," the apostle Paul links the Father's foreknowledge to *predestination*; predestination to *calling*; calling to *justification*; and justification to *glorification* –

an unbroken chain stretching from eternity past to eternity future (Rom. 8:29-30).

1 John 4:2-3 – "This is how you know the Spirit of God: Every spirit [person claiming divine gifting for service] that confesses that Jesus Christ has come in the flesh is from God, but every spirit that does not confess Jesus is not from God. This is the spirit of the antichrist, which you have heard is coming; even now it is already in the world."

John is writing against the Docetics, adherents of an early form of Gnosticism who deny the humanity of Christ, who maintain that Jesus only appeared to take on a body. The apostle counters this by insisting that Christl is both divine and human; to deny either His deity or His humanity is to deny His appearing as the God-Man. Such a claim renders Christ's finished work on the cross worthless.

In this call to sound doctrine, John says we will know if a person truly possesses the *indwelling* Spirit of God if he or she affirms both the deity and the humanity of Jesus. The Father has not sent the false prophet who disputes the Incarnation.

SUMMARY

Hopefully, this chapter has opened our eyes to the divine tapestry of the Trinity's work of salvation. Yes, Jesus is our Savior. He, and only He, took on human flesh and bore our sins on the cross. He, and only He, rose physically from the dead to secure everlasting life for us. Yet, Jesus didn't act alone.

In collaboration with the Father and the Spirit, Jesus volunteers to temporarily set aside His privileged position at the Father's right hand and come to earth to rescue us from sin. The Father is in full agreement with this. After all, He is the one who sends Jesus (John 6:38). The Father also takes an active role in our redemption as the one who foreknows, elects, and predestines us.

The Spirit – whom both the Father and the Son send – comes to call us to salvation, to regenerate us, indwell us, baptize us spiritually, sanctify us, and seal us. The Spirit also serves as the agent through whom believing sinners are adopted as children of the Father and made coheirs with Christ.

One day, when Jesus returns, His followers are glorified, or fully conformed to the image of Christ. And we enjoy everlasting life in the face-to-face presence of the Father, Son, and Holy Spirit.

Apart from the three persons of the Trinity, and their collaborative work of salvation, we would still be dead in our sins and without hope of being restored to a right relationship with God. Christ is our indescribable gift (2 Cor. 9:15), whom the Father sends and the Spirit signifies. The triune God is worthy of all our praise.

REVIEW

1. The Bible clearly teaches that Jesus is our _____, and salvation is found in no one else. And yet, as in the Trinity's work of _____, no single _____ of the Godhead acts alone. The Father, Son, and Holy Spirit all play important, complementary _____ in saving us from sin and restoring us to a right relationship with God.

2. Ephesians 1:3-14 is a good illustration of a Trinitarian expression of _____:

- In verses 3-6, Paul praises the Father for _____ us.
- In verses 7-12, he exalts Jesus for _____ for us.

- And in verses 13-14, he honors the Spirit for _____ us.

3. Simply stated, salvation is God's _____ for the sin that has ruined everything and alienated everyone from Him. For followers of Jesus, salvation is experienced as an everlasting, unbreakable _____ with Him. It has both temporal and eternal benefits. For example:

(a) We are *foreknown*, *elected*, and _____ in eternity past.

(b) Within our earthly lifetimes, God *calls* us to Himself; _____ us, or makes us spiritually alive; *justifies* us, or _____ us in right standing before Him; *indwells* us, or takes up permanent _____ in our human spirits; _____ us in the Holy Spirit, or places us positionally into the church; *sanctifies* us, or sets us apart and begins the _____ of making us more like Christ; _____ us into His family; and *seals* us, or places His mark of _____ on us.

(c) One day, the final act of salvation is completed in _____. We are physically resurrected and given incorruptible bodies similar to the resurrected body of our Savior.

4. There are seventy-five Trinitarian references in the New Testament. One of these is Ephesians 2:18, in which Paul states, "For through him [_____] we both [Jews and Gentiles] have access in one _____ to the _____." (ESV).

5. Apart from the three persons of the Trinity, and their _____ work of salvation, we would still be _____ in our sins and without hope of being restored to a right relationship with God. Christ is our indescribable _____, whom the Father sends and the Spirit signifies. The triune God is worthy of all our _____.

THINK

Questions for personal or group study

1. Various Christian sects and cults embrace Jesus as Savior while denying the doctrine of the Trinity. How do the following beliefs undermine a biblical understanding of salvation:

- Jehovah's Witnesses deny the deity of Christ. They believe Jesus of Nazareth was a sinless man who died on a torture stake and then, three days later, was *spiritually* (not physically) raised from the dead as an exalted archangel.
- Latter-day Saints believe the death and resurrection of Jesus secured *general salvation* – or resurrection – for nearly everyone, giving us the opportunity to work toward our own divinity, just as Heavenly Father, who once was a man, earned his exalted place as the god of this world.
- United Pentecostals believe the Father, Son, and Holy Spirit are three different manifestations of the same person.

2. In what ways can we rightly say that our salvation is past, present, and future?

3. Read Romans 8:29-30. Identify each of the following links in the "golden chain of redemption" as before time, in time, or beyond time:

Link	Before time	In time	Beyond time
Foreknowledge			
Predestination			
Calling			
Justification			
Glorification			

4. In the following Trinitarian passages, see if you can identify the saving work that each member of the Godhead performs. (Note: In some cases, two or more persons are credited with the same outcome.)

Passage	Father	Son	Holy Spirit
Romans 5:1-6			
Romans 8:14-17			
1 Corinthians 6:9-11			
2 Corinthians 1:21-22			
Ephesians 2:18			
2 Thessalonians 2:13-14			
Titus 3:4-7			
Hebrews 10:29-30			
1 Peter 1:1-2			
1 John 4:2-3			

5. How does a proper understanding of the Trinity enrich your personal relationship with Jesus Christ?

CHAPTER ELEVEN

The Trinity and Scripture

We know the Bible as the Word of God. That means God is the source of Scripture, revealing truths we are incapable of knowing without divine help. The Bible is *special revelation* in that it is a record of God's work before time, in time, and beyond time, with a particular emphasis on creation, sin, redemption, and restoration. As such, Scripture complements God's *general revelation*, which all people witness in creation and conscience (Rom. 1:18-32; 2:14-16).

In the Bible, God is revealed as one being in three persons – Father, Son, and Holy Spirit. These divine persons are co-equal and co-eternal. While they carry out distinct roles in creation and salvation, they are unified in purpose. As we have seen throughout this study, no single member of the Trinity acts alone. The holy, loving, self-giving persons of the Godhead set the standard for how human beings created in God's image should relate to God and to one another. At the same time, without Scripture, we would not be able to comprehend God as a Trinity.

Our ability to observe the natural world points us to a divine Designer. Yet, nature itself cannot adequately explain how Yahweh is one being in three persons. And mankind's universal conscience – for example, the understanding that torturing babies for fun is always wrong in all cultures at all times – compels us to conclude that there is a divine moral Law Giver. Even so, conscience can't tell us the reason behind or the remedy for our violations of standards that have been written on our hearts. It takes special revelation from this divine Designer and divine moral Law Giver. That's where the Bible steps into the picture.

The forty men who penned the Scriptures over a period of fifteen hundred years insisted that their message came from God, often at the cost of persecution, or even martyrdom. They claimed to be under the direction of the Holy Spirit (2 Sam. 23:2; 2 Pet. 1:20-21). The prophets ascribed their message to God. "Thus saith the Lord," "God said," "the Word of the Lord came to me," and similar phrases are found hundreds of times in the Bible. The apostle Paul declares, "All Scripture is inspired by God" (2 Tim. 3:16). Even before the New Testament canon is completed, Peter refers to the writings of Paul as "Scriptures" (2 Pet. 3:16). And ancient non-Christian writings attest to the truthfulness of the eyewitness accounts of Jesus of Nazareth.

In the previous two chapters, we saw how the Father, Son, and Holy Spirit worked collaboratively in creation and salvation. So, it should come as no surprise that the triune Godhead also produced the Word of God. Christians understand the Holy Spirit to be the divine agent of God's written revelation. Passages such as 2 Timothy 3:16 and 2 Peter 1:20-21, which we examine shortly, lead us to this conclusion. Yet the Spirit moved in concert with the Father and the Son.

Let's begin with a look at divine inspiration.

SCRIPTURE IS GOD-BREATHED

The apostle Paul writes in 2 Timothy 3:16-17, "All Scripture is inspired by God and is profitable for teaching, for rebuking, for correcting, for training in righteousness, so that the man of God may be complete, equipped for every good work."

The phrase "inspired by God" translates the Greek word *theopneustos*. It means "God-breathed" and conveys the idea that Scripture is the product of a holy exhalation. God did not breathe *into* the Scriptures, thus inspiring them; He breathed *out* His Word. The Bible's origin is God.

Theologian Charles Ryrie defines inspiration as "God's superintendence of the human authors of Scripture so that using their own individual personalities, they composed and recorded without error His revelation to man in the words of the original autographs."[1]

By superintendence, we do not mean that God dictated His Word to human stenographers, as Muhammad claimed of the Qur'an (via the angel Gabriel). Rather, God breathed out His Word, enabling the human authors to use their own writing styles, backgrounds, experiences, and ideas to put in written form the very thoughts of God, thus ensuring their accuracy.

We should be clear that inspiration applies directly and without qualification to the *autographs* of Scripture – that is, the original documents – not to subsequent manuscript copies, which contain some scribal errors, or to Bible translations, which vary in accuracy and readability. At the same time, we should take heart in knowing that we have a treasure trove of ancient manuscript copies that help ensure reliable and faithful representations of the inspired texts.[2]

Unalterable Oracles

God is so identified with His Word that when Scripture speaks, God speaks. For example, Paul writes, "For the Scripture tells Pharaoh, I raised you up for this reason so that I may display my power in you and that my name may be proclaimed in the whole earth" (Rom. 9:17; cf. Exod. 9:16).

Further, Scripture is called "the very words of God" (Rom. 3:2) and can neither be altered nor broken (Matt. 5:17-18; John 10:35; Rev. 22:18-19).

Note several important components that contribute to the inspiration of Scripture:

- The Holy Spirit's superintendence of the human authors guarantees an *inerrant* and *infallible* original text. Inerrancy means freedom from errors or untruths. Infallibility means the original manuscripts are incapable of error because God is wholly dependable. Inerrancy and infallibility may be distinguished but not separated. Inerrancy explains the truthfulness of Scripture, while infallibility explains the faithfulness of the One who inspired Scripture.
- Inspiration extends not just to spiritual ideas or theological concepts, but also to the very words of the writers. This is known as *verbal inspiration*.
- Finally, inspiration pertains to *all* Scripture. All parts of the Bible are equally authoritative. This is called *plenary inspiration*.

What Inspiration is Not

To promote a proper understanding of inspiration, let's take note of several false concepts with respect to the source of Scripture. In other words, we should understand that inspiration is not:

- Natural. The Bible is not the product of human will or genius, comparable to the plays of Shakespeare or the music of Mozart.
- Mystical. The human authors were not merely guided in the same way that others after them

wrote great religious works like *The City of God* or *The Pilgrim's Progress*; this diminishes Paul's meaning of "God-breathed."
- Layered. No part of Scripture is more inspired than others.
- Partial. All Scripture is inspired, even the genealogies and the record of sinful human deeds.
- Conceptual. The very words, not merely the ideas, are inspired.
- Dictation. God did not dictate messages to human scribes, who then mechanically transcribed them.

But *how* did God inspire His Word? Inspiration in some respects is a mystery because Scripture does not explain specifically how it occurred. The apostle Peter offers a hint when he writes, "No prophecy of Scripture comes from the prophet's own *interpretation*, because no prophecy ever came by the will of man; instead, men spoke from God as they were *carried along* by the Holy Spirit" (2 Pet. 1:20-21, emphasis added).

The word "interpretation" comes from the Greek *epilusis*. It conveys the idea of setting free or unleashing something. Therefore, with regard to Scripture, no human being may take credit for untethering divine revelation; God is the one who makes the meaning of the text accessible to human beings.

In addition, the phrase "carried along" translates a Greek term sometimes applied in a nautical context, describing the effect of wind on a ship's sails. As John MacArthur writes, "Similarly, the Spirit moved on the Biblical writers to produce the Word of God in the language of men."[3]

GOD SPEAKS

Let's survey a sampling of Bible passages that show how the Father, Son, and Holy Spirit work together to give us the Scriptures.

The Father

Consider just a few of the dozens of people to whom the Father speaks directly. In these verses, the Father either is implied as the speaking member of the Trinity, or the context identifies Him as such:

- Cain: "Then the Lord said to Cain …" (Gen. 4:6-16)
- Noah: "God said to Noah …" (Gen. 6:13-21)
- Job and his friends: "Then the Lord answered Job …" (Job 38:1 – 42:8)
- Abimelech: "But God came to Abimelech in a dream by night and said …" (Gen. 20:3-7)
- Moses and Aaron: "Then the Lord spoke to Moses and Aaron …" (Exod. 6:13; the Book of Exodus is filled with conversations between Yahweh and Moses)
- Samuel: "Then the Lord called to Samuel …" (1 Sam. 3:4-14)
- David: "The Lord answered David …" (1 Sam. 23:2)
- Solomon: "At Gibeon, the Lord appeared to Solomon in a dream at night. God said …" (1 Kings 3:5-14)
- Elijah: "Suddenly, the word of the Lord came to him [Elijah, in a cave], and he said to him …" (1 Kings 19:9-18)[4]
- Isaiah: "Then I heard the voice of the Lord asking

..." (Isa. 6:8-13)
- Ezekiel: "The word of the Lord came directly to the priest Ezekiel ..." (Ezek. 1:3)
- Jesus and His followers at Jesus' baptism: "This is my beloved Son, with whom I am well pleased" (Matt. 3:13-17)
- Peter, James, and John on the Mount of Transfiguration: "This is my beloved Son, with whom I am well pleased. Listen to him!" (Matt. 17:1-7)
- Andrew and Philip: "Then a voice came from heaven, 'I have glorified it [God's name], and I will glorify it again'" (John 12:20-28)

These examples don't begin to capture all the times and ways the Father speaks in the Bible. Moreover, His spokesmen frequently make it clear that the words being recorded are God's words, not the words of mere mortals. For example, Joshua tells the Israelites, "Come closer and listen to the words of the Lord your God" (Josh. 3:9). And 2 Kings 17:13 records, "Still, the Lord warned Israel and Judah through every prophet and every seer, saying, 'Turn from your evil ways ...'"

As the Father speaks, and as He takes ownership of His words, the Holy Spirit ensures that they are recorded for our benefit as the inerrant and infallible words of God.

The Son

Although Jesus doesn't leave us with words He penned, He speaks and acts in ways that become Scripture when faithful eyewitnesses record them. And He makes it clear He is working in concert with the Father and the Spirit. For example, Jesus claims to be sent by the Father: "For I have come down from heaven, not to do my own will, but the will of him who sent me" (John 6:38). In addition, Jesus casts out demons by the power of the Holy Spirit: "And if I drive out demons by the Spirit of God, then the kingdom of God has come upon you" (Matt. 12:28).

Further, Jesus claims equality with the Father: "I and the Father are one" (John 10:30; see also John 5:18). He claims not only to speak the truth, but to *be* truth incarnate: "I am the way, the truth, and the life. No one comes to the Father except through me" (John 14:6).

At the same time, Jesus confirms the inspiration and authority of the Hebrew Scriptures. He tells His listeners in the Sermon on the Mount, "Don't think that I came to abolish the Law or the Prophets. I did not come to abolish but to fulfill. For truly I tell you, until heaven and earth pass away, not the smallest letter or one stroke of a letter will pass away from the law until all things are accomplished" (Matt. 5:17-18).

In defense of His deity, Jesus tells the Jews who wish to stone Him, "If he [the Father] called those whom the word of God came to 'gods' – and *the Scripture cannot be broken* – do you say, 'You are blaspheming' to the one the Father set apart and sent into the world, because I said: I am the Son of God?" (John 10:35-36, emphasis added).

Jesus repeatedly claims to speak the truth, and no falsehood ever is found in Him. In order to be divine, Jesus could not misspeak, lead astray, or deceive. When Jesus speaks, He declares the very words of God – not merely in the sense of a prophet proclaiming the oracles of God, but as God Himself. Even so, He is careful to let us know that His words are fully consistent with those of the other members of the Trinity. He tells us that the words He speaks are not His own, but the words of His Father (John 12:49-50).

Perhaps the greatest argument in support of the inspiration, inerrancy, and infallibility of Scripture comes from Jesus' consistent affirmation of the Old Testament. Consider a few examples from the law, the prophets, and the writings:

The Law

Having been led by the Holy Spirit into the wilderness, Jesus repels each of Satan's temptations with a quote from Deuteronomy (Matt. 4:4 / Deut. 8:3; Matt. 4:7 / Deut. 6:16; Matt. 4:10 / Deut. 6:13).

In the Sermon on the Mount, Jesus quotes liberally from the Torah, seeking to restore the spirit of the law to a generation squinting through a thick cloud of human tradition (Matt. 5:21 / Exod. 20:13; Matt. 5:27 / Exod. 20:14; Matt. 5:31 / Deut. 24:1; Matt. 5:33 / Num. 30:2; Matt. 5:38 / Exod. 21:23-25).

Discussing divorce, Jesus takes His listeners back to the creation story (Matt. 19:4-6 / Gen. 1:27; 2:24).

He instructs the rich young ruler from the Torah (Matt. 19:17-20 / Exod. 20:12-16; Lev. 19:18; Deut. 5:16-20).

He challenges the Sadducees' denial of the resurrection by taking them back to the writings of Moses (Matt. 22:31-32 / Exod. 3:6).

He replies to an inquiry about the greatest of the six hundred and thirteen commandments in the Torah by leading His listeners back to Deuteronomy 6:5: "Love the Lord your God with all your heart, with all your soul and with all your strength."

And when the Pharisees accuse Jesus of testifying about Himself, without the required second witness, He replies, "Even in your law it is written that the testimony of two witnesses is true. I am the one who testifies about myself, and the Father who sent me testifies about me" (John 8:17-18 / Deut. 17:6).

The Prophets

In the synagogue in Nazareth, Jesus is invited to speak on the *Haftarah*, a selection from the books of Nevi'im

("Prophets") read publicly as part of the weekly religious practice. As He reads from Isaiah 61:1-2, a Messianic passage, He boldly proclaims, "Today, as you listen, this Scripture has been fulfilled" (Luke 4:21).

When Jesus is questioned about the wisdom of eating with tax collectors and sinners, He challenges His listeners to harken to the words of Hosea: "Go and learn what this means: I desire mercy and not sacrifice. For I didn't come to call the righteous, but sinners" (Matt. 9:13 / Hos. 6:6).

After an imprisoned John the Baptist sends disciples to inquire whether Jesus truly is the promised Messiah, Jesus tells the crowds about John and Himself: "What then did you go out to see? A prophet? Yes, I tell you, and more than a prophet. This is the one about whom it is written: See, I am sending my messenger ahead of you; he will prepare your way before you" (Matt. 11:9-10 / Mal. 3:1). God is the one speaking in Malachi 3. His "messenger" (John the Baptist) is sent to exhort the people to repent and prepare for God's "Messenger of the covenant" (Jesus), who is divine and yet a distinct person from God (see Mal. 3:1-5).

In Mark 7, the Pharisees and some of the scribes take issue with Jesus and His disciples for eating bread without first engaging in ceremonial washing. Responding to their insistence on manmade traditions, Jesus replies, "Isaiah prophesied correctly about you hypocrites, as it is written: This people honors me with their lips, but their heart is far from me. They worship me in vain, teaching as doctrines human commands" (Mark 7:6-7 / Isa. 29:13).

After observing the Passover on the night of His betrayal, Jesus quotes from Zechariah to prophesy the scattering of His disciples like sheep: "Tonight all of you will fall away because of me, for it is written: I will strike the shepherd, and the sheep of the flock will be scattered" (Matt. 26:31 / Zech. 13:7).

Just before heading to the Garden of Gethsemane, Jesus

identifies Himself with the Suffering Servant of Isaiah 52:13 – 53:12: "For I tell you, what is written must be fulfilled in me: And he was counted among the lawless. Yes, what is written about me is coming to its fulfillment" (Luke 22:37 / Isa. 53:12).

The Writings

The Old Testament writings include the Psalms, Proverbs, and a number of other books such as Ecclesiastes, Job, and Song of Solomon. Jesus quotes extensively from these as well.

In Matthew 21, the crowds in Jerusalem acclaim Jesus as "the Son of David." Even the children gathered at the temple shout, "*Hosanna* to the Son of David!" Indignantly, the chief priests and scribes protest to Jesus, asking, "Do you hear what these children are saying?" Jesus replies, "Yes, have you never read: You have prepared praise from the mouths of infants and nursing babies?" (Matt. 21:15-16 / Ps. 8:2).

Not long after His triumphant entry into Jerusalem, Jesus tells the parable of the vineyard owner as a warning of impending judgment on the nation of Israel. A great reversal of fortune is coming, when the church supplants Israel as God's agent of the kingdom, and when the apostles are the foundation stones of the New Jerusalem. Even more important, the humble Suffering Servant becomes the victorious King. Jesus then applies one of the Hallel Psalms – recited at Passover and other occasions – to Himself: "Then what is the meaning of this Scripture: The stone that the builders rejected has become the cornerstone?" (Luke 20:17 / Ps. 118:22).

While teaching in the temple, Jesus quotes from Psalm 110 to illustrate that the Messiah is more than a descendant of David – He is David's Lord: "David himself says by the Holy Spirit: The Lord declared to my Lord, 'Sit at my right hand until I put your enemies under your feet.' David himself calls him 'Lord'; how then can he be his son?" (Mark 12:36-37 / Ps. 110:1).

After washing His disciples' feet, Jesus quotes from Psalm 41 to implicate Judas as His betrayer: "I'm not speaking about all of you; I know those I have chosen. But the Scripture must be fulfilled: The one who eats my bread has raised his heel against me" (John 13:18 / Ps. 41:9).

As Jesus prepares His disciples for His work on the cross and subsequent return to the Father, He reminds them that hatred and persecution await them for their loyalty to Christ. Those who hate Jesus also hate His Father: "But this happened so that the statement written in their law might be fulfilled: They hated me for no reason" (John 15:25 / Ps. 35:19; 69:4).

Finally, on the cross, as the one who knew no sin became sin for us (2 Cor. 5:21), Jesus writhes in agony as He experiences the full weight of the Father's wrath: "About three in the afternoon Jesus cried out with a loud voice, *'Eli, Eli, lema sabachthani?'* that is, 'My God, my God, why have you abandoned me?'" (Matt. 27:46 / Ps. 22:1).

We could cite many other examples.[5] But it's clear that Jesus upholds the authority of the Hebrew Scriptures and applies many of them to Himself and His earthly mission to redeem fallen people. Equally important, Jesus' very words *become* Scripture, as He speaks and assures His followers that the Holy Spirit will bring to their minds everything He has taught them (John 14:26). In so doing, Jesus affirms the inspiration and authority of the New Testament in advance of its writing.

The Word was God

One final thought about the Son of God should not escape us. Jesus does even more than affirm the Hebrew Scriptures, reveal New Testament truth through His words and deeds, and assure His followers that the Holy Spirit will guide them into all truth. He doesn't just proclaim the Word of God; He *is* the Word of God.

As the apostle John records, "In the beginning was the Word, and the Word was with God, and the Word was God" (John 1:1). "Word" is the English rendering of the Greek *Logos*. It also may be translated "speech," "principle," or "thought." In Greek philosophy, it referred to a universal, divine reason, or the mind of God.

In John 1, there is no question that the apostle identifies Jesus as the *Logos*, establishing that He is eternal, with God (the Greek word translated "with" means face-to-face intimacy), and is, in fact, God. John goes on in verses 2-3 to establish Jesus as the Creator of "all things," meaning He cannot be a created being or a lesser god.

The Christian website GotQuestions.org notes: "*Logos* is used in many ways, yet in John's Gospel *Logos* is a clear reference to Jesus, the God who both created us and lived among us. *Logos* became a theological term important to Christians in the early church and remains a concept of significant influence today."[6]

The triune God not only gives us the Word of God; the second person of the Trinity *is* the Word of God – deity in human skin, showing us exactly who God is, while identifying with sinful and fallen people as He experiences humanity. Truly, "The Word became flesh and dwelt [literally "tabernacled"] among us. We observed his glory, the glory as the one and only Son from the Father, full of grace and truth" (John 1:14).

In summary, we should remember that Jesus claimed to be the Messiah, the Son of God, and the Son of Man (Matt. 16:16-18; 26:63-64; John 8:58). He was confirmed by acts of God (John 3:2; Acts 2:22) and declared that He had been given all authority in heaven and on earth to rule and to judge

(Matt. 28:18; John 5:22). Therefore, His views on the Bible are extremely important.

What did Jesus have to say? Norman Geisler writes, "Jesus declared that the Old Testament was *divinely authoritative* (Matt. 4:4, 7, 10); *imperishable* (Matt. 5:17-18); *infallible* (John 10:35); *inerrant* (Matt. 22:29; John 17:17); *historically reliable* (Matt. 12:40; 24:37-38); *scientifically accurate* (Matt. 19:4-5; John 3:12); and *ultimately supreme* (Matt. 15:3, 6)."[7]

The Holy Spirit

The Holy Spirit is the primary agent through whom the Scriptures came to us. He superintended the thoughts and words of the prophets and apostles so that what they wrote were the very words of God. We already have looked at 2 Timothy 3:16-17 and 2 Peter 1:20-21. These two passages are key to our understanding of the Bible as the breathed-out Word of God given to men directed by the Holy Spirit.

But in addition to these verses, the Bible reveals other ways the Holy Spirit works in concert with the Father and the Son to confirm biblical truths. A few examples:

Ezekiel 2:1-2 – "He [the Lord] said to me, 'Son of man, stand up on your feet and I will speak with you.' As he spoke to me, the Spirit entered me and set me on my feet, and I listened to the one who was speaking to me."

The same Spirit of God that energizes the chariot wheels (Ezek. 1:12, 19; 10:16-17) now enters Ezekiel and supplies the strength needed to carry out his prophetic ministry. This same Spirit superintends the prophet's words as they are recorded in the book bearing his name. The Spirit appears along with "the likeness of the Lord's glory" (1:28). Perhaps this is a rare vision of the preincarnate Christ. Or, at the very least, it's a veiled view of Yahweh on His heavenly throne.

Matthew 10:19-20 – Jesus tells His apostles, "But when they hand you over, don't worry about how or what you are to speak. For you will be given what to say at that hour, because it isn't you speaking, but the Spirit of your Father is speaking through you."

As Jesus braces His apostles for the world's hatred and persecution, He assures them that "the Spirit of your Father" will give them the words to speak. And the Spirit does just that as He indwells them (John 14:17), fills them (Acts 4:8), and testifies about Jesus through them (John 15:26-27).

Mark 13:11 – In a passage similar to Matthew 10:19-20, Jesus says to His apostles, "So when they arrest you and hand you over, don't worry beforehand what you will say, but say whatever is given to you at that time, for it isn't you speaking, but the Holy Spirit."

John 16:7-11 – Jesus tells His disciples, "Nevertheless, I am telling you the truth. It is for your benefit that I go away, because if I don't go away the Counselor will not come to you. If I go, I will send him to you. When he comes, he will convict the world about sin, righteousness, and judgment. About sin, because they do not believe in me; about righteousness, because I am going to the Father and you will no longer see me; and about judgment, because the ruler of this world has been judged."

When Jesus sends the Holy Spirit, He brings many wonderful benefits to the believer: regeneration, indwelling, Spirit baptism, sealing, and sanctification, to name a few.[8] At the same time, He has a ministry to the unbelieving world. He convicts unbelievers of the sin of unbelief – their rejection of God's provision for their sins in the person of Jesus Christ. He further convinces them of their puny manmade righteousness by laying it beside the perfect righteousness of Christ, in whose righteousness the believing sinner is clothed. And finally, the Spirit convicts unbelievers of the judgment that awaits them if they persist in rejecting the Son of God: the same destiny that awaits Satan, namely, the lake of fire (Matt.

25:41; Rev. 20:10). In all of this, the Spirit bears testimony of the Father and the Son.

John 16:13-15 – Jesus assures His followers, "When the Spirit of truth comes, he will guide you into all the truth. For he will not speak on his own, but he will speak whatever he hears. He will also declare to you what is to come. He will glorify me, because he will take from what is mine and declare it to you. Everything the Father has is mine. This is why I told you that he takes from what is mine and will declare it to you."

Here, we see the Holy Spirit working in perfect harmony with the Father and the Son to guide Jesus' followers so that their words are the very words of God. The *CSB Study Bible* notes, "The Spirit's ministry of guiding Jesus's followers into **all the truth** will fulfill the psalmists' longing for divine guidance (Ps. 25:4-5; 43:3; 86:11; 143:10). Isaiah recounted how God led his people in the wilderness by the Holy Spirit (Isa. 63:14) and predicted God's renewed guidance in the future (Isa. 43:19)."[9]

Romans 8:14-16 – "For all those led by God's Spirit are God's sons. You did not receive a spirit of slavery to fall back into fear. Instead, you received the Spirit of adoption, by whom we cry out, '*Abba*, Father!' The Spirit himself testifies together with our spirit that we are God's children, and if children, also heirs – heirs of God and coheirs with Christ – if indeed we suffer with him so that we may also be glorified with him."

The indwelling Holy Spirit bears witness that followers of Jesus are adopted sons and daughters of the Father and coheirs with Jesus of all things. This includes sharing in the sufferings of Jesus – and the wonder of future glorification.

Hebrews 3:7-11 – "Therefore, as the Holy Spirit says: Today, if you hear his voice, do not harden your hearts as in the rebellion, on the day of testing in the wilderness, where your fathers tested me, tried me, and saw my works for forty years. Therefore I was provoked to anger with that generation and said, 'They always go astray in their hearts, and they have not known my ways.' So I swore in my anger, 'They will not enter my rest.'"

The writer of Hebrews quotes from Psalm 95 and attributes the words to the Holy Spirit. Together, the psalmist and the voice of Yahweh make it clear that if the punishment for disobedience of the law was severe, then the penalty for rejection of the gospel would be far worse.

SUMMARY

The Bible we hold in our hands is a gift from the triune God. It is special revelation from the Father, Son, and Holy Spirit, telling us who they are, who we are, what's wrong with the world, and what God has done, is doing, and will do about it. Where the Bible speaks, God speaks. And there is more.

While the Bible was completed some two thousand years ago and survives in thousands of well-preserved manuscript copies, we may take comfort in knowing that the Bible is not merely a collection of fragile historical documents kept in climate-controlled archives. It is very much alive, as the writer of Hebrews declares: "For the word of God is living and effective and sharper than any double-edged sword, penetrating as far as the separation of soul and spirit, joints and marrow. It is able to judge the thoughts and intentions of the heart" (Heb. 4:12).

Think about it: Even though the last of the Scriptures was committed to writing nearly two thousand years ago, the God who breathed out His Word continues to speak to us through it.

His Word guides us, convicts us of sin, comforts us, grounds the truth in history, warns us, points us to Jesus, and tells us how the world ends. No other book makes the claims of the Bible, and no other book – not the Qur'an, the Book of

Mormon, or any other allegedly inspired writings – can stand the tests of history, archaeology, textual criticism, prophetic fulfillment, or the power to change human hearts. God has revealed Himself to all people in creation and conscience. What's more, the triune Godhead has collaborated to deliver a love letter to humanity through the miracle of the incarnate Word of God.

REVIEW

1. The Bible is _____ revelation in that it is a record of God's work before time, in time, and beyond time, with a particular emphasis on creation, sin, redemption, and restoration. As such, Scripture complements God's _____ revelation, which all people witness in creation and conscience. While creation points to a divine _____ and conscience implies a divine moral Law _____, it takes Scripture to enable us to comprehend God as a _____.

2. With respect to the Bible, the phrase "inspired by God," found in 2 Timothy 3:16, comes from the Greek word _____. It means "God-breathed" and conveys the idea that Scripture is the product of a holy _____. God did not breath *into* the Scriptures, thus inspiring them; He breathed _____ His Word. The Bible's origin is God.

3. The Father, Son, and Holy Spirit work together to give us the Scriptures. In the Old Testament, the _____ speaks directly to dozens of people, including Cain, Noah, Moses and _____, Elijah, Isaiah, and Ezekiel. Jesus affirms the complete reliability of the Old Testament by quoting many times from the

law, the _____, and the writings. And the Holy Spirit serves as the primary _____ of divine inspiration as He "carries along" the human authors in their writing (2 Pet. 1:20-21).

4. Although Jesus doesn't leave us with words He penned, He speaks and acts in ways that become _____ when faithful eyewitnesses record them. And He makes it clear He is working in _____ with the Father and the Spirit. For example, Jesus claims to be _____ by the Father (John 6:38). And He casts out demons by the _____ of the Holy Spirit (Matt. 12:28).

5. While the Bible was completed some two thousand years ago, we may take comfort in knowing that it is not merely a collection of fragile historical _____ kept in climate-controlled archives. It is very much _____, as the writer of Hebrews declares: "For the word of God is living and effective and _____ than any double-edged sword, penetrating as far as the separation of soul and _____, joints and marrow. It is able to judge the thoughts and _____ of the heart" (Heb. 4:12).

THINK

Questions for personal or group study

1. Which of the persons of the Trinity is identified as a contributing author of Scripture in the following passages:

(a) Exodus 6:13

(b) 2 Samuel 23:2

(c) Matthew 17:1-7

(d) John 5:24

(e) John 12:49-50

(f) 2 Peter 1:20-21

---

2. It's important to know what divine inspiration is and is not. Mark the following statements true or false:

(a) True / False – The Holy Spirit's superintendence of the human authors of Scripture guarantees an *inerrant* and *infallible* original text.

(b) True / False – The Bible is inspired in the same sense that great works of art, like Shakespeare's plays and Mozart's music, are inspired.

(c) True / False – The spiritual teachings of the Bible are true, but not necessarily the historical and scientific references.

(d) True / False – Inspiration pertains to *all* Scripture. All parts of the Bible are equally authoritative. This is called *plenary inspiration*.

(e) True / False – God dictated His Word to forty human authors, who served as little more than mechanical scribes.

3. Why is it important that Jesus quotes extensively from the three main sections of the Old Testament: the law, the prophets, and the writings?

4. How would you distinguish the Bible as the "Word of God" from Jesus as "the Word" (*Logos*) as depicted in John 1:1-18? What do the Bible and Jesus have in common as "the Word"?

5. Consider John 14:25-26. In what ways do the words of Jesus ensure that the New Testament, which was yet to be written, will be inspired, inerrant, and infallible?

While conservative evangelical scholars agree that the Son submits to the Father, and the Holy Spirit ministers as He is sent by both the Father and the Son, they disagree whether subordination is eternal or temporary.

CHAPTER TWELVE

Subordination and Scripture

Throughout this study, we have seen that the Bible reveals one true God in three persons: Father, Son, and Holy Spirit. These divine persons are co-equal and co-eternal. Put another way, the Father, Son, and Holy Spirit are God in the same way, and all are equally God. There is no difference in substance, essence, or being.

And yet we find Jesus submitting to the Father, being sent by the Father, learning obedience to the Father, and declaring that the Father is greater than He is. We also see the Father and the Son sending the Holy Spirit, who doesn't speak on His own, and who bears testimony of Jesus.

If the three persons of the Trinity are fully and equally divine, how can it be said that any one person of the Godhead submits to another? This thorny issue, which we have saved for last, centers around the doctrine of *subordination*. While conservative evangelical scholars agree that the Son submits to the Father, and the Holy Spirit ministers as He is sent by both the Father and the Son, they disagree whether subordination is *eternal* or *temporary*. This has sparked a vigorous debate in recent decades – a debate to which we return after briefly surveying how the Bible addresses subordination with respect to Jesus and the Holy Spirit.

JESUS AND SUBORDINATION

Jesus is one person with two distinct, but undivided, natures: human and divine (see Chapter Seven). This means, at least in part, that by adding sinless humanity to His deity, Jesus did not become less than co-equal with the other members of the Trinity.

At the same time, we must address several verses of Scripture that seem to say Jesus is a lesser being than God. Those who promote this false view of Jesus, and who use these particular Scriptures to support their position, are known as *ontological subordinationists*. They believe Jesus is less than God by nature of who Jesus is. Rather than the eternal Son of God, Jesus either is a created being, a lesser god, or both.

Ontological subordination should not be confused with *relational subordination*, a biblically faithful position also known as *economic* or *functional subordination*. According to relational subordination, the three persons of the Godhead are equal in nature, but they voluntarily submit to each other respecting the roles they play in creation and salvation. We should embrace relational subordination and reject ontological subordination.

Counterfeit Christian groups like the Jehovah's Witnesses reject Christ's deity. Instead, they believe Jesus is subordinate in nature or essence to the Father. The Watch Tower Bible and Tract Society insists that Jesus is the first of Jehovah's creations, namely, Michael the archangel. The Society also teaches that Michael was refashioned as Jesus the man two thousand years ago. Then, after His death on a torture stake, He was spiritually raised as an exalted Michael the archangel and taken to heaven. These views have no basis in Scripture.

However, ontological subordinationists point to the Bible to "prove" their points.

Key Passages

The following Bible verses often are quoted to buttress the claim that Jesus is lower in nature than the Father.

John 14:28 - "the Father is greater than I."

Jesus utters these words to His disciples gathered in the upper room, not to imply that He is inferior in nature to the Father. Quite the contrary. On many other occasions, Jesus places Himself on the same divine footage as Yahweh (e.g., John 5:17; 8:58; 10:30). Here, Jesus speaks of the Father being greater than He is because, in the Incarnation, Jesus has humbled Himself and taken on the form of a servant (see Phil. 2:5-8).

As Kenneth Samples writes, "By relinquishing the prerogatives of deity and veiling his divine glory, Jesus had, as a man, taken a role or position that was less than the Father in rank but certainly not in essence."[1]

John 20:17 - "I am ascending to my Father and your Father, to my God and your God."

Jesus speaks these words to Mary Magdalene after His resurrection. How could Jesus call the Father "my God" if Jesus is God Himself? The answer is quite simple. As the God-Man, Jesus possesses two natures: divine and human.

Having just been resurrected as glorified humanity – the divine nature does not die and therefore needs no resurrection – it is quite natural for Jesus to speak this way. He also provides assurance to Mary that He is the *firstfruits* of those who have fallen asleep; that is, He is the first to rise from the dead in a glorified body, never to die again. Paul expands on this thought in his first letter to the Corinthians (see 1 Cor. 15:20-22).

1 Corinthians 11:3 – "God is the head of Christ."

In this passage, Paul teaches Corinthian believers about relational authority within the Godhead, not degrees of nature. Earlier in the passage, Paul notes that the head (authority) of woman is man, even though Paul elsewhere stresses the equality of all people (see Gal. 3:28). Men and women are equal in being, as people God made to be His image bearers. As a result, all people share a common dignity and moral worth.

Rather than undermine the equality of persons in the Trinity, this verse shows that relational subordination is consistent with equality of being. Jesus voluntarily submits to the Father. This makes Him no less divine.

Colossians 1:15 – "the firstborn over all creation."

Ontological subordinationists lean on this verse to argue that Jesus had a beginning and thus is a created being. However, in this context, the word "firstborn" (Greek *prototokos*) does not mean the first one born (or created). If Paul had meant "first-created," as Jehovah's Witnesses contend, Paul could have used the Greek term *protoktisis* (first-created).

While *prototokos* can be rendered "firstborn" and used to identify a first-born child, it often means first in rank, an heir, or a preeminent one. In this respect, Jesus, who created all things (John 1:3; Col. 1:16), is sovereign over all He has made.

Voluntary Submission

The four passages of Scripture we just surveyed do not teach that Jesus is a lesser god, or a created being. Rather, they help broaden our view of what the Incarnation is all about. As the eternal Son of God, Jesus does not forfeit His deity in order to come to us in human flesh as Redeemer.

He voluntarily submits to the will of the Father, sets aside His privileged position at the Father's right hand, and adds sinless humanity to His deity. In His role as Suffering Servant (see Isa. 52:13 – 53:12), Jesus acknowledges that the Father is "greater" than He is – not better, nor more divine.

THE HOLY SPIRIT AND SUBORDINATION

If the Father sends Jesus, and Jesus willingly submits to the Father, what can we say about the Holy Spirit, whom both the Father and Jesus send (John 14:26; 16:7)? Is the Spirit a lesser deity? An impersonal force?

Jehovah's Witnesses, who say Jesus is a lesser divine being than Jehovah, also maintain that "holy spirit" is an impersonal force Jehovah uses to accomplish His will. Latter-day Saints have a more complex view. They sometimes distinguish between the Holy Ghost and the Holy Spirit, also called the "Spirit of Christ" and the "Light of Christ." The Holy Ghost is a deified person who occupies the premortal spirit realm. He is a "personage of Spirit"[2] who can be only one place at a time.[3] However, the Spirit "fills the immensity of space and … is everywhere present. This other Spirit is impersonal and has no size, nor dimensions…. We should speak of the Holy Ghost as a personage as 'he' and this other Spirit as 'it' …"[4]

However curious these views may be, they are unbiblical. The Bible is clear that the Holy Spirit (or Holy Ghost, depending on your English version of the Bible; they are references to the same person) is eternal, uncreated, personal, and divine. At the same time, the Holy Spirit is sent into the world for certain tasks: to testify of Jesus, to convict the unbelieving world, and to apply certain divine redemptive works to the lives of believers. Among these works are regeneration, indwelling, Spirit baptism, sanctification, sealing, and adoption.

The ministry of the Holy Spirit is neither coerced by other members of the Godhead, nor carried out impersonally, like electricity supplying power to light a darkened room. Rather, the Spirit works eternally with the other members of the

Godhead to carry out their cooperative works of creation, redemption, and restoration.

Key Passages

Let's look briefly at several passages of Scripture that describe the Spirit working in subordination to the Father and/or the Son.

John 14:16-17 – Jesus tells His followers, "And I will ask the Father, and he will give you another Counselor [Advocate, Comforter] to be with you forever. He is the Spirit of truth."

In these verses, Jesus informs us that the Holy Spirit is personal ("He"), of like mind and purpose with the Father and the Son ("another Counselor"), eternal ("with you forever"), and, like Jesus, not just truthful, but "the Spirit of truth." Thus, Christ reveals the deity and personality of the Holy Spirit.

John 14:26 – Jesus says, "But the Counselor, the Holy Spirit, whom the Father will send in my name, will teach you all things and remind you of everything I have told you."

When the Father sends the Holy Spirit in the name of Jesus, the Spirit continues the teaching ministry of Jesus, bringing to the disciples' minds a clear recollection of their Master's words and deeds. In so doing, the Spirit ensures a faithful body of Christian doctrine that endures today (2 Tim. 3:16; 2 Pet. 1:20-21).

John 16:7 – Jesus assures His disciples, "It is for your benefit that I go away, because if I don't go away the Counselor will not come to you. If I go, I will send him to you."

Not only does the Father send the Holy Spirit in Jesus' name, Jesus sends the Spirit after completing the work of redemption and returning to heaven to sit at the Father's right hand. Again, Jesus stresses the personhood of the Spirit, using the pronoun "him."

John 16:13-15 – Jesus promises, "When the Spirit of

truth comes, he will guide you into all the truth. For he will not speak on his own, but he will speak whatever he hears. He will also declare to you what is to come. He will glorify me, because he will take from what is mine and declare it to you. Everything the Father has is mine. This is why I told you that he takes from what is mine and will declare it to you."

Here, Jesus outlines the ministry of the Holy Spirit after the Spirit's arrival on the Day of Pentecost. The Spirit guides Jesus' followers into the truth. He speaks in harmony with the Father and the Son, hearing from the other persons of the Godhead and revealing their truth. He gives Christ's followers a glimpse into the future redemptive work of God. He glorifies Christ, applying Jesus' finished work on the cross in many and varied works of redemption – from regeneration and indwelling to Spirit baptism and adoption. And He has the full authority of the Godhead to declare gospel truth.

2 Corinthians 5:5 – Writing about our heavenly dwelling, Paul notes, "Now the one who prepared us for this very purpose is God, who gave us the Spirit as a down payment."

The Holy Spirit seals us, or marks us as belonging exclusively to God (2 Cor. 1:21-22; Eph. 1:13-14; 4:30). This is the Godhead's "earnest money" toward our heavenly home. As the Spirit dwells permanently in the temples of our bodies (1 Cor. 3:16; 6:19), He assures us that the good work God began in us will be completed (Phil. 1:6).

It's clear from these passages that the Holy Spirit is both divine and personal. We also may note that:

- Jesus asks the Father, who sends the Spirit.
- The Father sends the Spirit in Jesus' name.
- Jesus sends the Spirit.
- God (probably a reference to the Father, but it could be the triune Godhead) gives followers of

Jesus the Spirit as a down payment on our home in heaven.
- The Spirit does not speak on His own; He glorifies Jesus, who shares everything with the Father.

Placing these verses in a wider New Testament context, we see that the Holy Spirit is God (see Acts 5:3-4), even though He subordinates Himself to the Father and the Son in order to engage in redemptive work. He also is called the Spirit of God (Matt. 3:16), the Spirit of the Father (Matt. 10:20), and the Spirit of Christ (Rom. 8:9).

So, when we look at the three persons of the Trinity, we understand that they share an undivided divine nature, yet Jesus and the Holy Spirit take on subordinate roles in relation to the Father in order to carry out the Godhead's redemptive work.

TWO VIEWS OF RELATIONAL SUBORDINATION

With this understanding of relational subordination in mind, let's return to the issue raised at the start of this chapter: Has Jesus *always* submitted to the Father, or only during His earthly ministry? Put another way, did the Incarnation set in motion a temporary state in which the Son of God placed Himself under the authority of the Father? Similarly, did the Holy Spirit *eternally* submit to the will of the Father and the Son? Or, did the Day of Pentecost begin a finite period of time in which the Spirit submitted to the Father and the Son in order to be the agent of numerous saving works of God?

These are challenging questions about which conservative evangelical Christians disagree. There are two basic schools of thought. Some contend that an *eternal hierarchy* exists within the Godhead: The Father is supreme, and the Son and Holy Spirit obey, and have always obeyed, the Father's commands. Others maintain that an *eternal equality in authority* exists: The

Father, Son, and Holy Spirit possess equal authority with one another, with the Son and Spirit temporarily submitting to the Father for the purpose of carrying out a specific mission that the persons of the triune Godhead established through a covenant of redemption in eternity past.

While this is a vigorous debate, we should note that proponents of both views agree that the Bible depicts the Trinity as one true God (being) who exists as three distinct, but inseparable, co-equal, co-eternal persons: Father, Son, and Holy Spirit. All are God in the same way, and all are equally God. There is no difference in substance, essence, or being.

Further, both parties hold to the divine inspiration, inerrancy, infallibility, and sufficiency of Scripture. They agree about the full deity of the Son of God, to which He added full humanity in the Incarnation. They also believe in the physical resurrection of Jesus, the deity and personhood of the Holy Spirit, and salvation by grace alone, through faith alone, in Christ alone. But they take different views with respect to the relative authority of the three persons of the Trinity.

With these commonly held orthodox beliefs as a backdrop, let's briefly explore two competing views of subordination.

Eternal Hierarchy

The first view may be called the *eternal hierarchy* view. It's also known as the "gradational view" because its proponents maintain there is an eternal hierarchy of authority among the three persons.[5] According to this view, the Father is the supreme member of the Trinity. He possesses the highest authority, while the Son and the Holy Spirit are subordinate to Him and submit to His authority. This is how the three persons have related throughout eternity, including during the earthly ministry of Jesus and the present ministry of the Holy Spirit. It's also how the three members of the Godhead continue to relate into eternity future. Yet there remains an eternal equality of being among the three persons. That is, none of the members of the Godhead ever becomes less divine.

Theologian Bruce Ware refers to the eternal hierarchy view as the "authority-submission" structure in which "the three Persons understand the rightful place each has. The Father possesses the place of supreme authority, and the Son is the eternal Son of the eternal Father. As such, the Son submits to the Father, just as the Father, as eternal Father of the eternal Son, exercises authority over the Son. And the Spirit submits to both the Father and the Son. This hierarchical structure of authority exists in the Godhead even though it is eternally true that each Person is fully equal to each other in their commonly possessed essence."[6]

As Ware explains it, while each person of the Godhead is equal to the others in deity and attributes, the three persons are not equal in authority. Consequently, as the roles of the three persons are unique, so are their relationships with one another. The relationship between the Father and the Son is different than the relationship between the Father and the Spirit, or between the Son and the Spirit.

These functional and relational differences are seen in the creative and redemptive works of the triune God, according to theologian Wayne Grudem. For example, in creation, God the Father was the originator who "spoke the creative words to bring the universe into being," while God the Son was the executor "who carried out these creative decrees."[7] In the work of redemption, God the Father planned our salvation and sent the Son into the world. Jesus then obeyed the Father and completed the work of redemption, and the Holy Spirit was sent by the Father and the Son to apply redemption to us.[8]

Grudem concludes that "the different functions that we see the Father, Son, and Holy Spirit performing are simply outworkings of an eternal relationship between the three persons, one that has always existed and will exist for eternity.... These distinctions are essential to the very nature of God himself, and they could not be otherwise."[9]

There are several arguments in support of this position:

The biblical evidence. For example, we see the Father choosing us in the Son before the foundation of the world (Eph. 1:3-4). Further, this subordination continues into eternity future, where in the end the Son turns over everything to the Father and is subject to Him (1 Cor. 15:28).

The teachings of the early church. The creeds seem to support such a view with statements such as "eternal generation (or eternal begetting) of the Son," "begotten of the Father before all worlds," and "The Son is of the Father alone: not made, nor created, but begotten."[10]

The immutability of God. If Yahweh does not change (Mal. 3:6), and if Jesus is the same yesterday, today, and forever (Heb. 13:8), then the persons of the Trinity must always have existed in the same relationships with one another – along with the same lines of authority.

The distinction between the persons of the Trinity. If the Father, Son, and Holy Spirit may be distinguished, what is the basis of this? It can't be based on their essence, since all three persons possess the same nature and attributes. Therefore, they must be distinguished based on their unique relationships with one another, which their different roles determine.

In summary, the eternal hierarchy view upholds the equality of persons within the Godhead, while maintaining that unique relationships exist, and have always existed, between the three persons. Within these relationships, the Father, in His supremacy, prescribed eternal functions for the Son and the Holy Spirit.

Temporary Hierarchy

An opposing view is the *temporary hierarchy* view, sometimes referred to as the "equivalence view."[11] It holds that the Father, Son, and Holy Spirit are eternally equal in authority and essence. The Son temporarily engaged in what's known as *functional subordination* for the purpose of carrying out His role as the Lamb of God who takes away the sin of the world (John 1:29).

In a similar manner, the Holy Spirit is temporarily engaged in an earthly ministry of testifying about Jesus, drawing unbelievers to Christ, and regenerating, indwelling, baptizing, sealing, and sanctifying those who follow Jesus. However, when the work of redemption is complete, the Son and the Spirit resume their full co-equal authority with the Father.

In support of this view, the late theologian Benjamin Warfield points out that the word "son" speaks of equality, not dependence. He notes that the primary meaning of "son" is likeness, which can be seen in the Jews' interpretation of Jesus' self-designation as the Son of God as a claim to deity or equality with God.[12] As the apostle John writes, "This is why the Jews began trying all the more to kill him [Jesus]: Not only was he breaking the Sabbath, but he was even calling God his own Father, making himself equal to God" (John 5:18).

Further, proponents of the temporary hierarchy view note that the terms Father, Son, and Holy Spirit are not the exclusive names for the members of the Trinity. Jesus and the biblical writers employ a variety of names, titles, and descriptions for the persons of the Godhead. Paul, for example, frequently uses God, Lord, and Spirit to describe the Father, Son, and Holy Spirit.

With respect to the Father, Scripture describes Him with many names and titles: "*Abba*" (Papa – Gal. 4:6); "Alpha and Omega" (Rev. 1:8); "the Ancient of Days" (Dan. 7:9); "God

Most High" (Gen. 14:18-20); "the everlasting God, the Creator" (Isa. 40:28); "The Lord Is My Banner" (Exod. 17:15); "my shepherd" (Ps. 23:1); "the Lord of Hosts" (James 5:4); and many more.

Regarding Jesus, dozens of titles are ascribed to Him, such as "the Alpha and the Omega" (Rev. 22:13); "the source and protector of our faith" (Heb. 12:2); "the bread of life" (John 6:35); "a great high priest" (Heb. 4:14); "judge of the living and the dead" (Acts 10:42); "Lamb of God" (John 1:29); "the Lion from the tribe of Judah" (Rev. 5:5); "the spiritual rock" (1 Cor. 10:4); "Savior" (Luke 2:11); "the way" (John 14:6); "the Word" (John 1:1); "the true vine" (John 15:1); and more.

In a similar way, Jesus and the biblical authors use a variety of terms to depict the Holy Spirit: "Counselor" (John 14:16); the one who convicts the world of sin, righteousness, and judgment (John 16:7-11); "seal" and "down payment of our inheritance" (2 Cor. 1:22; Eph. 1:14); "Spirit of truth" (John 16:13); "the Spirit of adoption" (Rom. 8:15); "the Spirit of God" (Matt. 3:16); "the Spirit of the Lord" (2 Cor. 3:17); "the Spirit of Christ" (1 Pet. 1:11); teacher (1 Cor. 2:13); the testifier (Rom. 8:16); and more.

In addition to all this, the common order in which Christians express the names of the members of the Trinity – Father, Son, and Holy Spirit – should by no means be used to support the notion of eternal subordination. Rather, the order of the Godhead is variable in the New Testament. For example, in the writings of Paul, the Son is mentioned first in sixteen lists, the Spirit first in nine, and the Father first in six.[13]

Paul writes in 2 Corinthians 13:14, "The grace of the Lord Jesus Christ, and the love of God, and the fellowship of the Holy Spirit be with you all." Peter lists the order as Father, Spirit, and Jesus Christ in 1 Peter 1:2. Jude refers to the Holy Spirit, God, and the Lord Jesus Christ (Jude 20-21). And in writing about the Holy Spirit's distribution of spiritual gifts, the apostle Paul writes, "Now there are different gifts, but the same Spirit. There are different ministries, but the same Lord [Jesus]. And there are different activities, but the same God [Father] produces each gift in each person" (1 Cor. 12:4-6).

It's also important to remember that many passages of Scripture attribute a certain action to one member of the Trinity, while another passage attributes that same action to a second or third divine person. For example:

- The Father elects, or chooses, persons for salvation (Rom. 8:29; 1 Pet. 1:2). Jesus chooses to reveal the Father to certain persons (Matt. 11:27). And the Holy Spirit then chooses which spiritual gifts to bestow on followers of Jesus (1 Cor. 12:11).
- The Father sends the Holy Spirit (John 14:16, 26), and so does the Son (John 15:26).
- Jesus offers access to the Father (John 14:6). Yet Paul writes that we have access to the Father by one Spirit (Eph. 2:18).
- Jesus sits in final judgment (Matt. 25:31-32; 2 Cor. 5:10), and so does God (Rom. 14:10). "God" could be a reference to Christ in His deity, or it could mean the judgment seat belongs to both the Father and the Son.
- Jesus intercedes for us (Rom. 8:34; Heb. 7:25), yet so does the Holy Spirit (Rom. 8:26-27).
- The Holy Spirit indwells the believer (1 Cor. 3:16; 6:19). Jesus also dwells in us (2 Cor. 13:5; Col. 1:27; Gal. 2:20), and the Son and the Spirit together reside in us (John 14:16-20; Rom. 8:9-11). Finally, Jesus speaks of the Father and the Son making their home in the believer's heart (John 14:23).

Other examples could be cited, but these Scriptures are sufficient to show how the three persons of the Godhead share a number of divine works. As Millard Erickson writes, "The various works attributed to the different persons of the Trinity are in fact works of the triune God. One member of the Godhead may in fact do this work on behalf of the three and be mentioned as the one who does that work, but all participate in what is done.... [T]he sending of the Son to earth was done by the Father but on behalf of the Trinity. In a very real sense, all of them sent the Son, and all had jointly decided that he would go. In the Atonement, the Son offers his life as a sacrifice to the Godhead, and the Father accepts it on behalf of the Godhead."[14]

Erickson goes on to write, "Although one person of the Trinity may occupy a more prominent part in a given divine action, the action is actually that of the entire Godhead, and the one person is acting on behalf of the three. This means that those passages that speak of the Father predestining, sending, commanding, and so on should not be taken as applying to the Father alone but to all members of the Trinity."[15]

Proponents of the temporary hierarchy view make much of the unity of the three persons. Loraine Boettner writes, "The Father is, and always has been, as much dependent on the Son as the Son is on the Father, for, as we need to keep in mind, self-existence and independence are properties, not of the Persons within the Godhead, but of the Triune God."[16] He further notes that "each of the Persons participates to some extent in the work of the others.... Hence we say that while the spheres and functions of the three persons of the Trinity are different, they are not exclusive. That which is done by one is participated in by the others with varying degrees of prominence."[17]

The plan of redemption, for example, involves a covenant in eternity past between the members of the Godhead. There is an agreed division of labor, with each person voluntarily assuming a particular part of the work. This involves temporary submission of the Son to the Father and of the Spirit to the Father and the Son, but not in such a way that renders any member of the Godhead inferior to the other.

In other words, while the Father, Son, and Holy Spirit take on different roles in the redemption of lost sinners, the full equality of the persons is preserved. We must be careful to distinguish between what's known as *functional subordination* and the *essential equality* of the members of the Trinity. To illustrate, when Jesus says, "the Father is greater than I" (John 14:28) and "I can do nothing on my own" (John 5:30), these are not admissions of inferiority but declarations of temporary functional subordination in the days of His flesh.

Last, we should note that this functional subordination is both *voluntary* and *temporary*. Jesus is neither coerced nor compelled to become a servant; He humbles Himself (see Phil. 2:5-8). It is more theologically accurate to speak of Jesus' *self-humiliation* than His subordination. As Gilbert Bilezikian stresses, "Nobody subordinated him and he was originally subordinated to no one."[18]

Equally important, Christ's humiliation is an interim or temporary state. Bilezikian continues, as he comments on Philippians 2:5-8, "It [the form of a servant] was something new for him. Being in the form of a servant was not an eternal condition. He took it up. He became obedient unto death. Prior to the incarnation there had been no need for him to be obedient since he was equal with God. But despite the fact that he had the dignity of sonship he learned obedience through what he suffered (Heb. 5:8). Obedience was a new experience for him, something he had to learn. It was not an eternal state."[19]

To summarize, the temporary hierarchy view agrees with the eternal hierarchy view in the nature and attributes of God, namely that there is one true God who exists as three distinct, but inseparable, co-equal, co-eternal persons: Father, Son, and Holy Spirit. Where the temporary hierarchy view differs from the eternal hierarchy view is that it sees Scripture describing a covenant of redemption in eternity past, in which the three persons of the Godhead agree to a voluntary and temporary subordination, with the Father sending the Son to be the Savior of the world, and the Father and Son sending the Holy Spirit as the agent of many redemptive works, including serving as the indwelling presence of Yahweh in the temple of the believer's body.

AVOIDING TEXT-JAM

As with other teachings of the Christian faith – from election to eschatology – the doctrine of subordination is an important secondary doctrine over which followers of Jesus may disagree without accusing one another of heresy. Functional subordination – whether it is eternal or temporary – is not one of the non-negotiables of the Christian faith, such as the essential truths of the Trinity, the deity and humanity of Christ in the Incarnation, salvation by grace alone, through faith alone, in Christ alone, and the inspiration and authority of Scripture. Rather, subordination is a deeper dive into the eternal relationship between the persons of the Godhead, and it deserves our attention. Good and godly evangelical theologians agree on the essential nature and attributes of the Trinity, while taking different views of the tenure each person holds in subordination.

A recurring problem arises when we examine divergent views of biblical doctrines. A proponent of one view may stack up an impressive list of biblical texts to support his or her view, and someone else may match it with a similar number of verses espousing an opposing view. Both may be wrong, but both cannot be right. So, how should we deal with what Kevin Giles calls "text-jam" – seeking to resolve complex theological issues by pitting one verse of Scripture against another?[20]

Giles points to Athanasius, the fourth-century theologian

whose orthodox view of Jesus prevailed over that of Arius, who insisted that Jesus was a lesser divine being, not the uncreated, co-equal, co-eternal Son of God. Athanasius noticed that Arius had compiled an impressive stack of biblical texts to buttress his heretical view. This led to the realization that any sufficiently clever theologian may "prove" almost any false doctrine by bending the biblical texts in a particular direction. We see this today, for example, with Jehovah's Witnesses, who either change the Scriptures, or twist them, to promote views of Jesus that generate a modern-day match for the heretical views of Arius.

According to Giles, Athanasius discovered that theology could only be carried out soundly when one has a profound grasp of the "scope" of Scripture – "the overall drift of the Bible, its primary focus, its theological center."[21] When applied to our understanding of Jesus, two clear truths emerge: "on the one hand, that the Son is eternally one in being and action with the Father and, on the other hand that the Son gladly and willingly subordinated himself temporarily for us and our salvation."[22]

So, how does all of this contribute to meaningful and biblically faithful explorations of difficult doctrines like subordination? A few observations may help:

Begin with clearly established truths. Proponents of the eternal hierarchy view and the temporary hierarchy view of subordination all embrace an orthodox understanding of the Trinity: one true God who exists as three distinct, but inseparable, co-equal, co-eternal persons – Father, Son, and Holy Spirit. Despite differences of opinion about the tenure of subordination, evangelical Christians on both sides of the debate stand in unity against heretical views of the Godhead, whether these come from Arius in ancient times or from counterfeit Christian groups in modern times.

In a similar manner, promoters of various views of eschatology far too often insist that their understanding of the order of events surrounding the return of Christ are spot on and non-negotiable. Whether they are correct in their particular view of last things overlooks the fact that nearly all evangelical Christians agree that Jesus today is seated at the right hand of the Father as our Mediator and Intercessor; that He is returning personally, visibly, and physically one day in power and great glory; that He will raise the dead and execute final judgment; and that He will create new heavens and a new earth to be enjoyed by all followers of Jesus – even those whose particular brand of eschatology turns out to be wrong.

Starting on common ground with fellow Christians is always a good idea that enhances unity and enables us to engage in lively, but respectful, debate as we seek to better understand the mysteries of God's Word.

Consider the context. A single verse of Scripture, while always true, never stands alone. Each verse is part of a larger thought, which fits into an entire book, thus contributing to the full canon of Scripture. For example, if we study Jesus' earthly ministry, we may quote John 11:35, where the apostle records, "Jesus wept." Without regard for context, someone may quote this verse to "prove" that Jesus was merely a human being, because, after all, God never cries. But this argument fails to take into account everything else Scripture says about Jesus. Yes, He was fully human, adding sinless humanity to His deity (John 1:14). Yes, He experienced a full range of human emotions, from anger to delight. Yes, He knew what it was like to be hungry, thirsty, lonely, and sad. Yes, He faced every sort of temptation we face. The Gospels and the epistles drip with the humanity of Jesus.

But the New Testament also proclaims His deity. It tells us He is the Creator of all; He is co-equal with the Father; He rightly may forgive sins and receive worship; and He displays the other attributes of deity. A full reading of Scripture discloses that Jesus is the eternal Son of God who, two thousand years ago, left His privileged position at the Father's right hand and stepped into time and space, adding sinless humanity to His deity via the miracle of the virgin birth. Further, as the God-Man, Jesus could pay an eternal debt owed to an eternal God, while being the substitutionary sacrifice for the sins of human beings.

Yes, Jesus wept at the tomb of Lazarus, a dear friend who suffered the common malady of mankind – the encroaching enemy of death. Yet, the story doesn't end with Jesus' tears. Instead, it reaches its zenith when the Son of Man encounters rotting flesh in an unsealed tomb and shouts, "Lazarus, come out!" Immediately, Jesus' dear friend stumbles into the light, struggling against his tightly wound grave clothes (John 11:43-44).

Many "proof texts" fall short of proving anything other than a false teacher's aversion to "rightly dividing the word of truth" (2 Tim. 2:15 KJV).

Don't solve God's mysteries. The Lord has revealed many once-hidden truths to us in Scripture: the Incarnation (1 Tim. 3:16); Christ in us, the hope of glory (Col. 1:27); Jews and Gentiles together as one body in Christ (Eph. 3:1-11); the seven stars and seven candlesticks (Rev. 1:12-20); the kingdom of heaven (Matt. 13:1-52); the translation of living saints (1 Cor. 15:51-57); Israel's blindness (Rom. 11:25); the church as the bride of Christ (Eph. 5:22-33); and more.

Yet it appears the Lord has kept some secrets to Himself, at least for now, and we run the risk of dividing the body of Christ when we claim to have solved the mysteries. For example, no one can name the day or the hour of Christ's return, but we all should be ready for it (Matt. 24:36-44). No one knows who the Antichrist is, but we all should understand that the spirit of antichrist has been alive and well for centuries (1 John 4:3). No one can achieve the wisdom or knowledge of God, yet we all should put on the mind of Christ by following His plainly revealed Word (Isa. 55:8-9; 1 Cor. 2:16; Phil. 2:5-8).

In a similar way, we should guard against being lifted up with pride as we go deeper into a knowledge of God's Word. We have mentioned the doctrines of election and eschatology earlier in the chapter – two secondary doctrines that often cause unnecessary division within the church. Not that these are trifling doctrines by any means. These are deep and wonderful doctrines about which much has yet to be learned.

The great nineteenth-century preacher, Charles H. Spurgeon, a fully Reformed pastor and theologian, proclaimed the truth of divine election without presuming to speak what God holds closely to the vest. In a sermon delivered August 1, 1858, he said:

> I see in one place, God presiding over all in providence; and yet I see, and I cannot help seeing, that man acts as he pleases, and that God has left his actions to his own will, in a great measure.
>
> Now, if I were to declare that man was so free to act, that there was no presidence of God over his actions, I should be driven very near to Atheism; and if, on the other hand I declare that God so overrules all things, as that man is not free enough to be responsible, I am driven at once into Antinomianism [the belief that there are no moral laws God expects Christians to obey] or fatalism.
>
> That God predestines, and that man is responsible, are two things that few can see. They are believed to be inconsistent and contradictory; but they are not. It is just the fault of our weak judgment. Two truths cannot be contradictory to each other.
>
> If, then, I find taught in one place that everything is fore-ordained, that is true; and if I find in another place that man is responsible for all his actions, that is true; and it is my folly that leads me to imagine that two truths can ever contradict each other.
>
> These two truths, I do not believe, can ever be welded

into one upon any human anvil, but one they shall be in eternity: they are two lines that are so nearly parallel, that the mind that shall pursue them farthest, will never discover that they converge; but they do converge, and they will meet somewhere in eternity, close to the throne of God, whence all truth doth spring.[23]

Spurgeon acknowledged the tension between divine sovereignty and human responsibility, and he proclaimed it without apology. Perhaps we can learn from this as we explore, and debate, important secondary doctrines such as relational subordination.

REVIEW

1. Concerning the doctrine of subordination, conservative evangelical scholars agree that the _____ submits to the Father, and the _____ _____ is sent by both the Father and the Son. Yet these scholars disagree whether subordination is _____ or _____. Despite holding different views, they all agree that the Bible reveals one true God in three _____: Father, Son, and Holy Spirit. These divine persons are God in the same way, and all are _____ God.

2. How would you explain the following verses to the person who cites them as "proof" that Jesus is a created being, a lesser god, or both:

(a) John 14:28 – "the Father is greater than I."

(b) John 20:17 – "I am ascending to my Father and your Father, to my God and your God."

(c) 1 Corinthians 11:3 – "God is the head of Christ."

(d) Colossians 1:15 – "the firstborn over all creation."

3. It's important to distinguish between *ontological subordination*, a false teaching that claims Jesus is a _____ being than God, and *relational subordination*, a biblically faithful position holding that the three persons of the Godhead are equal in _____, but they voluntarily

_____ to each other respecting the roles they play in creation and salvation.

4. The *eternal hierarchy* view of relational subordination argues that the Father is the _____ member of the Trinity. He possesses the highest authority, while the Son and the Holy Spirit are always subordinate to the Father and _____ to His authority. The *temporary hierarchy* view of relational subordination holds that the Father, Son, and Holy Spirit are eternally equal in _____ and essence. The Son and the Spirit, however, temporarily submitted to the Father for the purpose of carrying out their earthly ministries.

5. As with other teachings of the Christian faith – from election to eschatology – the doctrine of subordination is an important _____ doctrine over which followers of Jesus may _____ without accusing one another of heresy. Perhaps we should observe the following guidelines to engage in meaningful and biblically faithful explorations of these difficult doctrines:

Begin with clearly established _____.
Consider the _____.
Don't _____ God's mysteries.

THINK

Questions for personal or group study

1. Two Jehovah's Witnesses come to your door and share their beliefs about Jesus. As you know, Jehovah's Witnesses are *ontological subordinationists*. Specifically, they believe Jesus is the first of Jehovah's creations, namely, Michael the archangel. What

questions could you ask your visitors to challenge their unbiblical view that Jesus and Michael are the same being?

2. Why do you think the Holy Spirit tends to get less attention than God the Father and Jesus Christ? What are some ministries of the Holy Spirit that attest to His personality and His deity? How does He participate in the work of redemption?

3. We explored two views of relational subordination: the eternal hierarchy view and the temporary hierarchy view. Could you offer brief explanations of both views? What do supporters of each view hold in common with one another concerning the nature and attributes of the triune Godhead?

4. Which view of relational subordination – eternal hierarchy or temporary hierarchy – seems the most biblically faithful?

5. We noted that the debate over eternal vs. temporary hierarchy concerns a secondary doctrine. How would you distinguish between a so-called primary doctrine, which is a non-negotiable teaching of the Christian faith, and a secondary doctrine? Which of the doctrines listed on the next page would you consider primary (non-negotiable) or secondary – and which ones are neither (mark P for primary, S for secondary, N for neither).

P / S / N	Doctrine
	The Trinity – one true God in three co-equal, co-eternal persons: Father, Son, and Holy Spirit
	The virgin birth of Christ
	A church steeple with or without a cross
	Divine election
	The modes (immersion, pouring, sprinkling) and meaning of water baptism
	The church member who makes the best potato salad
	The full deity and full humanity of Jesus
	Requirements for local church membership
	Jesus' sacrificial and substitutionary death on the cross
	Salvation by grace alone, through faith alone, in Christ alone
	Carpet, tile, or vinyl in the fellowship hall?
	The inspiration and authority of Scripture
	The roles of women in church leadership
	Baptism in the Holy Spirit
	The physical resurrection of Jesus
	Eschatology (last things)
	Hymns or contemporary Christian music in worship?

CLOSING THOUGHTS

In *What Is the Trinity?*, R. C. Sproul notes that the church, throughout its history, has used the term *Trinity* to stop the mouths of heretics – those who teach tritheism (the idea that there are three gods), as well as those who deny the tri-personality of God by insisting on some view of Unitarianism. "We might say that the word *Trinity* is a 'shibboleth,'" he writes.[1]

If the word *shibboleth* isn't immediately familiar to us, Sproul points out its significance in the history of ancient Israel. The book of Judges records a conflict between the men of Gilead and the men of Ephraim. To identify their brothers, the soldiers of Gilead use a helpful password: *Shibboleth*. The Ephraimites are unable to pronounce this word, thus exposing them as enemies (Judg. 12:5-6). So, *shibboleth* has become a term for a test word by which someone's true identity may be ascertained.

For example, Sproul points out that the Dutch people employed a *shibboleth* during the German occupation of their country in World War II. They used the name of a resort town on the coast of Holland known as Scheveningen. While the Germans could speak Dutch and pass as Dutch people most of the time, they simply could not properly pronounce

Scheveningen. So, the Dutch used this name to root out German spies.

"The church should not hesitate to use certain words as shibboleths to force people to reveal where they stand on various issues," writes Sproul. He notes that J. I. Packer, noted Canadian theologian, identified *inerrancy* as one such *shibboleth*. If you want to know where someone stands with respect to Scripture, ask, "Where do you stand on inerrancy?" As Sproul concludes, "many people will choke on that word before they will affirm it."[2]

Trinity is an apt *shibboleth* we may use today to confirm orthodox views of God while weeding out misguided, or even heretical, views. The triunity of God accurately conveys what God has revealed about the Father, Son, and Holy Spirit in Scripture, and what the church has confessed historically about the essence and persons of the Godhead. As followers of Jesus, we should have a firm grasp on the doctrine of the Trinity, ready at all times to defend this biblical doctrine with gentleness and respect (1 Pet. 3:15-16).

NOTES

INTRODUCTION

1. LifeWay Research defines evangelicals as people who strongly agree with the following statements: (1) The Bible is the highest authority for what I believe; (2) It is very important for me personally to encourage non-Christians to trust Jesus Christ as their Savior; (3) Jesus Christ's death on the cross is the only sacrifice that could remove the penalty of my sin; (4) Only those who trust in Jesus Christ alone as their Savior receive God's free gift of eternal salvation. See Note 2 below for citation.

2. Ligonier Ministries, "The State of Theology in the United States," conducted by LifeWay Research, 2018, and reported in *Christianity Today*, https://christianitytoday.com/news/2018/october/what-do-christians-believe-ligonier-state-theology-heresy.html.

CHAPTER ONE: DEFINING THE TRINITY

1. J. I. Packer, *Concise Theology: A Guide to Historic Christian Beliefs* (Carol Stream, IL: Tyndale House Publishers, Inc., 1993), 40.
2. Freddy Davis, "Why Belief in the Trinity is Essential in Christianity – Part 1: Understanding the Concept of the Trinity," *Worldview Made Practical*, Vol. 10, No. 21, June 3, 2015, 1.
3. Davis, 2.
4. Nabeel Qureshi, *No God But One: Allah or Jesus?* (Grand Rapids, MI: Zondervan, 2016), 65.
5. *The Baptist Faith & Message* (Nashville, TN: LifeWay Press, 2000), 7.
6. Bruce A. Ware, *Father, Son, and Holy Spirit: Relationships, Roles, and Relevance* (Wheaton, IL: Crossway, 2005), 43.
7. Qureshi, 56.
8. Qureshi, 56.
9. Freddy Davis, "Why Belief in the Trinity is Essential in Christianity – Part 2: The Importance of the Doctrine of the Trinity," *Worldview Made Practical*, Vol. 10, No. 22, June 10, 2015, 1.
10. *Let God Be True* (New York: Watchtower Bible and Tract Society, 1952), 102.
11. "The Nicene Creed: Where it came from and why it still matters," https://zondervanacademic.com/blog/the-nicene-creed-where-it-came-from-and-why-it-still-matters/.
12. Millard J. Erickson, *Making Sense of the Trinity: Three Crucial Questions* (Grand Rapids, MI: Baker Academic, 2000), 18.
13. "The Nicene Creed: Where it came from and why it still matters," https://zondervanacademic.com/blog/the-nicene-creed-where-it-came-from-and-why-it-still-matters/.
14. Nathan A. Jacobs, "Understanding Nicene Trinitarianism," *Christian Research Journal*, Vol. 41, No. 4, 2018, 24.
15. Jacobs, 26.

16. The ideas in these paragraphs come largely from Jacobs, 25-26.

CHAPTER TWO: FALSE VIEWS OF THE TRINITY

1. The Qur'an erroneously assumes that Christians believe God acquired a son through sexual relations with Mary. See Qur'an 4:171; 5:72-75, 116.
2. John of Damascus, *On Heresies*, 83, cited in Nathan A. Jacobs, "Understanding Nicene Trinitarianism," *Christian Research Journal*, Vol. 41, No. 04, 2018, p. 22.
3. Matt Slick, "Tritheism," https://carm.org/tritheism.
4. From a dialogue with Robert M. Bowman Jr., author of *Why You Should Believe in the Trinity*, March 31, 2019.
5. James R. White, *The Forgotten Trinity: Recovering the Heart of Christian Belief* (Bloomington, MN: Bethany House Publishers, 1998), 153.
6. Matt Slick, "Modalism," https://carm.org/modalism.
7. Tertullian, *Against Praxeas*, 1.1; Gregory of Nyssa, *Against Eunomius*, 1.34, cited in Nathan A. Jacobs, "Understanding Nicene Trinitarianism," *Christian Research Journal*, Vol. 41, No. 04, 2018, 22.
8. "What is Unitarian Universalism?" https://gotquestions.org/unitarian-universalism.html.
9. "What is modalism / Modalistic Monarchianism?" https://gotquestions.org/Modalistic-Monarchianism.html.
10. Joseph R. Nally, Jr., "What is Polytheism?" http://reformedanswers.org/answer.asp/file/45596.
11. Ibid.
12. Jacobs, 25.
13. R. C. Sproul, *What Is the Trinity?* The Crucial Questions Series, No. 10 (Orlando, FL: Reformation Trust Publishing, 2011), 17.

14. "What is henotheism / monolatrism / monolatry?" https://gotquestions.org/henotheism.html.
15. The Doctrine and Covenants of The Church of Jesus Christ of Latter-day Saints (Salt Lake City, UT: The Church of Jesus Christ of Latter-day Saints, 1982), 130:22.
16. "Why Should I Follow God's Laws?" https://mormon.org/beliefs/god.
17. Jacobs, 22.
18. John of Damascus, *On Heresies*, 83, cited in Jacobs, 22.
19. Tertullian, *Against Praxeas*, 1.1; Gregory of Nyssa, *Against Eunomius*, 1:34, cited in Jacobs, 22.
20. Jacobs, 22.
21. Basil of Caesarea, *Epistle* 52.1, cited in Jacobs, 22.

CHAPTER THREE: ONE GOD

1. "How are idols connected to demons (Deuteronomy 32:16-17)?" https://gotquestions.org/idols-demons.html.
2. "Judaism 101," http://jewfaq.org/shemaref.htm.
3. The full passage is Deuteronomy 6: 4-9. The other two Scriptures are Deuteronomy 11:13-21 and Numbers 15:37-41.
4. J. I. Packer, *Concise Theology: A Guide to Historic Christian Beliefs* (Carol Stream, IL: Tyndale House Publishers, Inc., 1993), 42.
5. These unique qualities of God are explored more fully in Robert Morey's *The Trinity: Evidence and Issues* (Iowa Falls, IA: World Bible Publishers, Inc., 1996), 63-71.
6. For more on these Old Testament passages, see Millard J. Erickson, *Making Sense of the Trinity: Three Crucial Questions* (Grand Rapids, MI: Baker Academic, 2000), 29-34.
7. This is explored in more detail in Michael S. Heiser, *Angels: What the Bible Really Says About God's Heavenly Host* (Bellingham, WA, Lexham Press, 2018).
8. Qureshi, *No God But One*, 50-51.
9. Heiser, 11-13.

10. Heiser, 12.
11. Ibid.
12. G. Fisher and C. J. Woodworth, *Studies in the Scriptures, Vol. 7, "The Finished Mystery"* (New York, NY: Watchtower Bible and Tract Society, 1918), 410.

CHAPTER FOUR: THREE PERSONS

1. White, *The Forgotten Trinity*, 66-67.
2. Timothy Keller, *The Reason for God: Belief in an Age of Skepticism* (New York, NY: Penguin Books, 2008), 223.
3. Cornelius Plantinga Jr., *Engaging God's World: A Christian Vision of Faith, Learning, and Living* (Grand Rapids, MI: Wm. B. Eerdmans Publishing Co., 2002), cited in Keller, 224.
4. George M. Marsden, *Jonathan Edwards: A Life* (Yale University Press, 2003), 462-463.
5. Morey, *The Trinity*, 169.
6. Heiser, *Angels*, 57.
7. Rodrick K. Durst, *Reordering the Trinity: Six Movements of God in the New Testament* (Grand Rapids, MI: Kregel Publications, 2015), 66, 72.
8. Durst, 113.

CHAPTER FIVE: THE FATHER IS GOD

1. Morey, *The Trinity*, 251.
2. These five observations come from Morey, *The Trinity*, 270-272.
3. For more on this, see my resource, *What Every Christian Should Know About Salvation: Twelve Bible Terms That Describe God's Work of Redemption*.
4. *HCSB Study Bible* (Nashville, TN: Holman Bible Publishers, 2010), 1961.

5. Robert James Utley, *Paul Bound, the Gospel Unbound: Letters from Prison (Colossians, Ephesians and Philemon, Then Later, Philippians), Vol. 8*, Study Guide Commentary Series (Marshall, TX: Bible Lessons International, 1997), 74.
6. Michael Bauman, "God as Father," *Christian Research Journal*, Vol. 23, No. 2, online version, https://equip.org/article/god-as-father/#.

CHAPTER SIX: THE SON IS GOD

1. See 1 Enoch 46:1; 48:10; 4 Ezra 13.
2. Norman L. Geisler and Douglas E. Potter, *The Doctrine of Angels & Demons* (Indian Trail, NC: Norm Geisler International Ministries, 2016), 14-15.
3. John Calvin, *Institutes of the Christian Religion* (Peabody, MA: Hendrickson Publishers, 2008), n.p.
4. Herbert Lockyer, *All the Angels in the Bible* (Peabody, MA: Hendrickson Publishers, 1995), 87.
5. C. Fred Dickason, *Angels: Elect & Evil* (Chicago: Moody Press, 1974), 80-81.
6. "Teaching with Authority," https://ligonier.org/learn/devotionals/teaching-authority/.
7. Among my favorites are: *Putting Jesus in His Place: The Case for the Deity of Christ* by Robert M. Bowman and J. Ed Komoszewski; *The Deity of Christ* by John MacArthur; *The Historical Jesus* by Gary Habermas; *The Historical Jesus of the Gospels* by Craig S. Keener; and *Jesus and the Eyewitnesses: The Gospels as Eyewitness Testimony* by Richard Bauckham.
8. John MacArthur, *The Deity of Christ* (Chicago: Moody Publishers, 2017), 205.
9. Robert M. Bowman and J. Ed Komoszewski, *Putting Jesus in His Place: The Case for the Deity of Christ* (Grand Rapids, MI: Kregel Publications, 2007), 148.
10. MacArthur, 187-188.

11. William Barclay, *The Letters to the Philippians, Colossians, and Thessalonians*, rev. ed. (Louisville, KY: Westminster, 1975), 35.
12. Barclay, 35-36.
13. Bowman and Komoszewski, 84.
14. This is known as "Granville Sharp's Rule," which came along after the KJV but well before the NWT. Basically, the rule states that if you have two nouns, such as "God" and "Savior," the first with an article before it and the second without it, and they are connected by the word *and*, then both nouns describe the same object.
15. Bowman and Komoszewski, 149.
16. "Who Is Jesus Christ?" https://jw.org/en/publications/books/bible-study/who-is-jesus-christ/.
17. Eric J. Bargerhuff, *The Most Misused Verses in the Bible* (Bloomington, MN: Bethany House Publishers, 2012), 85.
18. F. F. Bruce, in *Inerrancy*, ed. Normal L. Geisler (Grand Rapids, MI: Zondervan, 1979).
19. James R. White, *Scripture Alone: Exploring the Bible's Accuracy, Authority, and Authenticity* (Bloomington, MN: Bethany House Publishers, 2004), 186-187.
20. "What is the doctrine of eternal Sonship and is it biblical?" https://gotquestions.org/eternal-Sonship.html.

CHAPTER SEVEN: JESUS AS THE GOD-MAN

1. Bruce Ware, *The Man Christ Jesus: Theological Reflections on the Humanity of Christ* (Wheaton, IL: Crossway, 2012), 26.
2. Eliza R. Snow, *Biography and Family Record of Lorenzo Snow* (Salt Lake City: Deseret News Co., 1884), 46-47. See also http://mormon.org/values/family.
3. C.S. Lewis, *Mere Christianity* (New York: Macmillan Publishing Company, 1952), 154.
4. Kenneth Richard Samples, *God Among Sages: Why Jesus Is Not*

Just Another Religious Leader (Grand Rapids, MI: Baker Books, 2017), 34.
5. Cited in Kenneth Richard Samples, *Without a Doubt: Answering the 20 Toughest Faith Questions* (Grand Rapids, MI: Baker Books, 2004), 61.
6. Wayne Grudem, *Systematic Theology: An Introduction to Biblical Doctrine* (Leicester, England: Inter-Varsity Press / Grand Rapids, MI: Zondervan Publishing House, 1994), 529.
7. Samples, *God Among Sages*, 37.
8. See Samples, *God Among Sages*, 37-38.
9. Samples, *God Among Sages*, 38-39.
10. Samples, *God Among Sages*, 44.
11. Gerald Bray, *God Is Love: A Biblical and Systematic Theology* (Wheaton, IL: Crossway, 2012), 439.
12. Samples, *God Among Sages*, 49-50. See also H. Wayne House, *Charts of Christian Theology and Doctrine* (Grand Rapids, MI: Zondervan Publishing House, 1992), 55-56; and Bruce Milne, *Know the Truth*: *A Handbook of Christian Belief* (Downers Grove, IL: InterVarsity Press, 2009), 142-145.
13. C. H. Spurgeon, "The Man of Sorrows," a sermon delivered March 2, 1873, at the Metropolitan Tabernacle, Newington, found at https://www.spurgeongems.org/vols19-21/chs1099.pdf.

CHAPTER EIGHT: THE HOLY SPIRIT IS GOD

1. White, *The Forgotten Trinity*, 140.
2. Freddy Davis, "Why Belief in the Trinity is Essential in Christianity: Part 4 – The Biblical Basis for the Trinity," *Worldview Made Practical*, Vol. 10, No. 24, June 24, 2015, 9.
3. *CSB Study Bible* (Nashville, TN: Holman Bible Publishers, 2017), 5.

CHAPTER NINE: THE TRINITY AND CREATION

1. White, *The Forgotten Trinity*, 106.
2. This explanation of Gnosticism comes mostly from White, *The Forgotten Trinity*, 106-109.
3. Kenneth Wuest, "Ephesians and Colossians," *Wuest's Word Studies in the Greek New Testament* (Grand Rapids, MI: Wm. B. Eerdmans Publishing Company, 1981), 183.
4. Marvin Richardson Vincent, *Word Studies in the New Testament*, Vol. 4 (New York: Charles Scribner's Sons, 1887), 380–381.
5. Robert Jamieson, A. R. Fausset, and David Brown, *Commentary Critical and Explanatory on the Whole Bible*, Vol. 1 (Oak Harbor, WA: Logos Research Systems, Inc., 1997), 17.
6. Andrew Knowles, *The Bible Guide*, 1st Augsburg books ed. (Minneapolis, MN: Augsburg, 2001), 22.
7. Morey, *The Trinity*, 198.
8. Erickson, *Making Sense of the Trinity*, 57.
9. Erickson, 66-67.

CHAPTER TEN: THE TRINITY AND SALVATION

1. Erickson, *Making Sense of the Trinity*, 15.
2. For a more detailed discussion of the doctrine of divine election, see Phillips, *What Every Christian Should Know About Salvation: Twelve Bible Terms That Describe God's Work of Redemption*.
3. Paul G. Humber, *400 Prophecies, Appearances, or Foreshadowings of Christ in the Tanakh (Old Testament)*, Associates for Biblical Research, http://biblearchaeology.org, 2012.
4. For a complete exploration of these seventy-five Trinitarian references, see Durst, *Reordering the Trinity: Six Movements of God in the New Testament*. Morey provides an abbreviated listing of

"The Economical Trinity" in *The Trinity: Evidence and Issues*, 441-442.
5. *ESV Study Bible* (Wheaton, IL: Crossway Bibles, 2008), 2265.
6. Jamieson, Fausset, and Brown, *Commentary Critical and Explanatory on the Whole Bible*, Vol. 2 (Oak Harbor, WA: Logos Research Systems, Inc., 1997), 434.

CHAPTER ELEVEN: THE TRINITY AND SCRIPTURE

1. Charles C. Ryrie, *A Survey of Bible Doctrine* (Chicago: Moody, 1972), 38.
2. Good resources for laypersons on the reliability of Scripture include: *Has God Spoken?* by Hank Hanegraaff; *Can We Still Believe the Bible?* and *The Historical Reliability of the New Testament* by Craig Blomberg; *In Defense of the Bible*, edited by Steven B. Cowan and Terry L. Wilder; *How We Got the Bible* by Neil R. Lightfoot; *Seven Reasons Why You Can Trust the Bible* by Erwin Lutzer; *Scripture Alone* by James R. White; and *Can We Trust the Gospels?* by Peter J. Williams.
3. "Is all Scripture inspired by God?" found at http://gty.org/resources/questions/QA171/is-all-scripture-inspired-by-god.
4. Robert Bowman notes that many Christian interpreters see these statements about "the word of the Lord" coming to a prophet (see also Ezek. 1:3) as part of the background for John's description of the preincarnate Son as "the Word" in John 1:1, 14.
5. Additional references may be found from Rich Robinson, "Jesus' References to Old Testament Scriptures," https://jewsforjesus.org/answers/jesus-references-to-old-testament-scriptures/.
6. "What is the Logos?" https://gotquestions.org/what-is-the-Logos.html.
7. Norman L. Geisler and Frank Turek, *I Don't Have Enough Faith to Be an Atheist* (Wheaton, IL: Crossway, 2004), 228.

8. For more on the many facets of salvation, see Phillips, *What Every Christian Should Know About Salvation: Twelve Bible Terms That Describe God's Work of Redemption.*
9. *CSB Study Bible* (Nashville, TN: Holman Bible Publishers, 2017), 1699.

CHAPTER TWELVE: SUBORDINATION AND SCRIPTURE

1. Samples, *God Among Sages*, 46.
2. Doctrine and Covenants (Salt Lake City, UT: The Church of Jesus Christ of Latter-day Saints, 1982), 130:22.
3. *Gospel Principles* (Salt Lake City, UT: The Church of Jesus Christ of Latter-day Saints, 2009), 32.
4. *Doctrines of Salvation*, comp. Bruce R. McConkie, 3 vols. (Salt Lake City, UT: Bookcraft, 1954-56), 1:49-50.
5. Millard J. Erickson, *Who's Tampering with the Trinity? An Assessment of the Subordination Debate* (Grand Rapids, MI: Kregel Publications, 2009), 17.
6. Bruce Ware, *Father, Son, and Holy Spirit: Relationships, Roles, and Relevance* (Wheaton, IL: Crossway, 2005), 21.
7. Grudem, *Systematic Theology*, 252.
8. Grudem, 249.
9. Grudem, 250-251.
10. Grudem, *Evangelical Feminism and Biblical Truth: An Analysis of More than One Hundred Disputed Questions* (Sisters, OR: Multnomah, 2004), 415-416.
11. Erickson, *Who's Tampering with the Trinity?*, 17.
12. Benjamin B. Warfield, "Trinity," *The International Standard Bible Encyclopedia*, ed. James Orr (Grand Rapids, MI: Eerdmans, 1952), 5:3020.
13. Kevin Giles, *Jesus and the Father: Modern Evangelicals Reinvent the Doctrine of the Trinity* (Grand Rapids, MI: Zondervan, 2006), 109-110.
14. Erickson, *Who's Tampering with the Trinity*, 135-136.

15. Erickson, 137-138.
16. Loraine Boettner, *Studies in Theology* (Philadelphia: Presbyterian and Reformed, 1964), 112.
17. Boettner, 118.
18. Gilbert Bilezikian, "Hermeneutical Bungee-Jumping: Subordination in the Godhead," *Journal of the Evangelical Theological Society 40*, No. 1 (March 1997), 59.
19. Bilezikian, 60.
20. Kevin Giles, *The Trinity and Subordinationism: The Doctrine of God and the Contemporary Gender Debate* (Downers Grove, IL: InterVarsity Press, 2002), 3.
21. Giles, *The Trinity and Subordinationism*, 3.
22. Ibid.
23. Charles H. Spurgeon, "Expositions of the Doctrines of Grace," http://spurgeon.org/sermons/0385.htm.

CLOSING THOUGHTS

1. R. C. Sproul, *What Is the Trinity?* The Crucial Questions Series, No. 10 (Orlando, FL: Reformation Trust Publishing, 2011), 93.
2. Sproul, 94.

ADDITIONAL RESOURCES

Other apologetics resources available from the MBC:

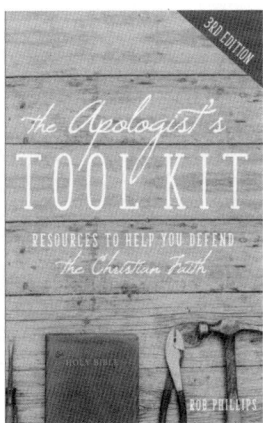

The Apologist's Tool Kit:
Resources to Help You Defend the Christian Faith

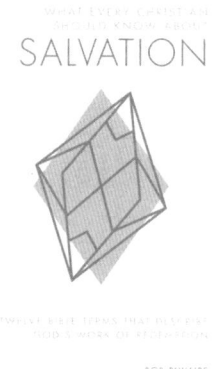

What Every Christian Should Know About Salvation:
Twelve Bible Terms That Describe God's Work of Redemption

The Last Apologist: A Commentary on Jude
for Defenders of the Christian Faith

ADDITIONAL RESOURCES • 249

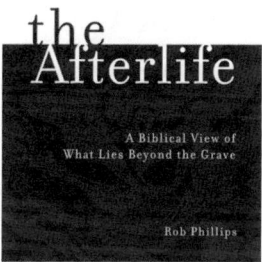

What Everyone Should Know About the Afterlife:
A Biblical View of What Lies Beyond the Grave

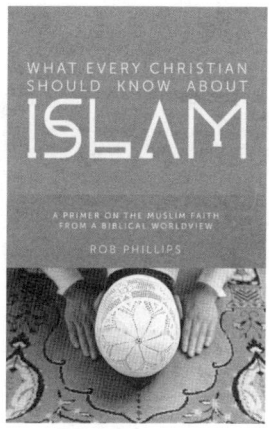

What Every Christian Should Know About Islam:
A Primer on the Muslim Faith from a Biblical Perspective

WHAT EVERY CHRISTIAN
SHOULD KNOW ABOUT

A BIBLICAL PRIMER
FOR THE LOCAL CHURCH

ROB PHILLIPS

What Every Christian Should Know About Same-sex Attraction:
A Biblical Primer for the Local Church

Order printed copies at mobaptist.org/apologetics
Print and Kindle editions available from Amazon